Balto Girl

Balto Girl

Janet Vanik Divel

ARCHWAY PUBLISHING

This book is a work of non-fiction. Unless otherwise noted, the author and the publisher make no explicit guarantees as to the accuracy of the information contained in this book and in some cases, names of people and places have been altered to protect their privacy.

Archway Publishing books may be ordered through booksellers or by contacting:

Archway Publishing
1663 Liberty Drive
Bloomington, IN 47403
www.archwaypublishing.com
844-669-3957

ISBN: 978-1-6657-2732-7 (sc)
ISBN: 978-1-6657-2733-4 (hc)
ISBN: 978-1-6657-2731-0 (e)

Library of Congress Control Number: 2022913412

Print information available on the last page.

Archway Publishing rev. date: 8/19/2022

CONTENTS

Acknowledgments and Credits

I wanted to start by giving a very special thanks to my friend Max Pollock. Several years back, I had a conversation with Max, and he said one encouraging word that resulted in me writing my story. Sometimes in life, all you need is a particular word from someone to get you going.

I am so grateful to my husband, Bill, for being my driver and guide on our trips to Baltimore and helping me acquire images for my book.

I also know that the encouragement from friends and family helped me thru this journey. Thanks to Deborah Lee Alt, Terri Bolander, Kathy Eagle, Dustin Ericksen, William Gribbon, Beverly Hayward (Rest in Peace), Jacquelyn Hodak and Anne Troise.

Thank you to all my contributors,

Alamy
Charles Alt
Baltimore Museum of Industry
Pam Berry
A.Aubrey Bodine
Sharen and Gary Coster
Joy Diehl Dougherty
Frank Durkee
Elaine Eff
Getty Photos
Christian Kendzierski (Archdiocese of Baltimore)
Kevin Koenig (Exchange Club of Highlandtown and Canton)
Josh Kohn (Creative Alliance)
Ron Legler (President of the Hippodrome)
Logue Family

Maryland Center for History and Culture
Paul McMullen (Catholic Review)
Henry Lewis Mencken
Kitty Parr
Chuck Robinson Photography
Vincent Scully
Spencer Stewart
Shutterstock

Chapter One

THE BALTIMORE
ROW HOUSE

PHOTO COURTESY OF AAUBREY BODINE

To explain Baltimore's uniqueness during the '40s, '50s, and the '60s, one must first know what a row house is. How did it become such a big success for the people of Baltimore at that time? The first noticeable thing would have been the front steps, mainly consisting of beautiful white marble – its real fame. Any day, during the week or weekend, people were out scrubbing with a scrub brush those steps with brown soap or Ajax scouring powder. The marble gave a richness and an artistic distinction to the entrance. Some houses had marble in their vestibules, the entrance area. They shared a party wall, a single wall between the two. Most of the homes in East Baltimore had skylights located on the second floor in the middle of the house. It would provide light and ventilation.

And they were challenging to reach since they were positioned over the stairway going upstairs. The little row house in this story had three small rooms downstairs; when entering the house, the stair steps were in front of view. Turn left, and there were small rooms, no separation. Standing at the front window and looking straight, there was a view directly to the back window. In the 1930s, the outhouse was at the bottom of the yard. The exterior bricks, red in color, came from local clay pits. There was no short supply of suitable clay. In 1847, thirteen Baltimore Quarries; produced the marble for the Washington Monument, eventually for the row house trim and steps. The builder who could not afford marble would paint the wooden steps white to give a similar marble effect. The row houses' width on the small street averaged thirteen feet and four inches, fourteen feet, and length of thirty feet. In our cities' early settlement, it was essential to get the most people to the least amount of space in a livable manner. They usually would have just built apartments with people piled horizontally; the row house was an old concept that seemed to work well in London and other European cities. The row house first appeared in Northern Europe. At the time, a large middle class was changing the concept of a home. They wanted a place that had its own front door. The row house was the perfect answer because it was practical and serviceable use of space. The lots were narrow but still allowed people to enter and have a small yard. It gave you a sense of pride and ownership. The houses in the picture below were fourteen feet wide. 400 block North Port Street faced 2400 block Jefferson street is also called an alley street. Early 1940's.

The historian Vincent Scully wrote a characterization stating that the beautiful streets with their marble steps were the perfect example of the row house. Everything about it was decisive; the height of the building's windows and the door just the right size for people to have space to live. The red brick of various shades gave the street a rhythm. His portrayal was spot-on. There is no better way to describe old Baltimore city with the spotless neighborhoods and the pride that existed together. Vincent Scully was born on August 21, 1920. He was an American art historian, born and raised in New Haven, Connecticut. and received his Ph.D. from Yale University in 1949. Taught classes at Yale in 1949 and was the most influential architectural teacher ever. His opinions were very significant, And he would regularly receive standing ovations. Vincent Scully died at age 97 on November 30, 2017, in Lynchburg, Virginia. Many compliments about Baltimore City design from many famous people thru the years and we can't forget the almost twin city, Philadelphia, Pennsylvania. Philadelphia was the older city that set the directions and guides for Baltimore to mimic. Philadelphian artisans looked at it with high confidence, and Baltimore derived its style from a row house, and later builders that came to Baltimore from Philadelphia created the Baltimore style. Early immigrants were collections of artisans, skilled workers, tradesmen, laborers, machinists, and journeymen, all educated in a European school or apprenticeship. When the Bohemians landed in Baltimore, most were equipped with a trade, like blacksmiths. The training in Europe started in their pre-teen years. The extent of house building was carried on by German-born or second-generation German builders. Many of the German immigrants to America in the second half of the nineteenth century were skilled woodworkers who found employment as cabinet-makers, carvers, piano-makers, and print-makers. Many of the Immigrants changed their trades to carpenters and house-builders. Most of the small-scale Builders were German-born and bred. At that time, thousands of Irish immigrant artisans came to Baltimore. One of the things that the Irish brought with them was their decorative plasterwork. Many other eastern and western Europeans also landed in the late 1800s, consisting of the Bohemians, Italian, Chinese, Jewish, and Polish ethnic groups. The larger home on the broader streets was usually for the well to do people, and the smaller-size homes on the smaller streets were for the not as fortunate as far as finances go. The houses were built differently than the row-type houses in New York, where in New York, the basement entrances were in the front under the access to the house. Baltimore row-houses basement entrances were in the back, and you could get to them thru the alley or a tunnel structure between dwellings. Neighborhoods were varied. There was a class difference by street with the height and width of the houses. People were generally not segregated by sharp outlines of the area or different styles of homes. At that time, the land was cheap, and the currency was scarce. The row houses were built as a block and would sell for anywhere from $450.00 to $850.00. The landowner allowed the builder who had the capital to build on it. He would rent or sell the houses. London had a similar system. Both the landowner and the builder made money. The buyer would not have to purchase the land, which cost him less to buy the house at low rates. More people could afford to purchase their own homes. The builder would charge, or whoever owns the land could charge ground rent every year. The rent was anywhere from $15.00 to $60.00 yearly. If the house owner fails to pay the ground rent, the landowner could repossess the home and the property. What a racket.

The loan amount usually consisted of the monthly installments of $30.00 to $40.00, in some cases more, but this included the price of the house, ground rent, taxes, and insurance. No Social Security or help from any government agency those days. You were entirely responsible for your home. Women were rarely on the deed. A man only buys title (perpetual lease) for land/house. The contract becomes personal property, and the wife's signature is not necessary so that he can sell it with just his name. Women rarely owned any real estate unless their spouse or a family member died and left it to her in their will. In 1929 Baltimore ranked 1st in homeowners among more prominent cities in the U. S. In 1894, row houses were beloved words. They were numerous, small, neat, and comfortable dwellings. Individuals of nearly every circumstance in life. Builders ornamented portions of the city. Handsome rows of such buildings and the bright door brasses, the clean steps, and well-washed windows – in short, the general air of neatness and comfort, which characterizes them, indicate peace, happiness, contentment, and similar virtues are their tenants. That was the plan. The photo below is part of the title to 408 North Port Street; even in 1961, there was still ground rent. When Madeline Vanik purchased the home after her mother, Elizabeth

Koerner, passed the annual ground rent of thirty dollars per year on the 1st days of April and October.

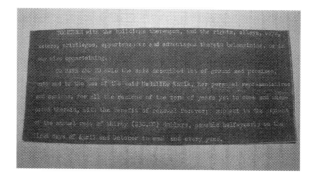

I can't forget the alleyways' uniqueness, and there was the use of a front entrance and a back entrance. The small back yards gave them a garden, maybe with a rose bush.

PHOTO COURTESY OF AAUBREY BODINE

East on Mulberry shows the backs of Brice Street 1945

The words Baltimore Charm City are from the writings of Henry Louis Mencken, an Editor, Author, Critic, and Scholar, born in 1880. There was something about the cleanliness of the vestibule, a small entrance hall, actually the entire house. It was their pride in the ownership, maybe old-fashioned thinking, being in that environment, their home was the end of the rainbow.

The house and the Neighborhood were their entire world. The immigrants worked hard for this, and they identified with it. For most of these refugees and their children, the home was the first objective of ownership in their new homeland, and this took years of sacrifice to accomplish. The realism of their thoughts is why the older generation fought for any changes affecting them. They grew up with a different mindset than us. Most started with just a suitcase or a cloth sack. Their heartache was yet to come. Most of the Neighborhood at that time was peaceful, comfortable world, but changing. Not to say it was perfect in every way; there were problems at times.

The decline of this very productive city took years. When World War 11 ended in the mid-40s, it was the start of the withdrawal of citizens looking for a new way of living in these city dwellers. The soldiers came home to a world of real estate developers buying land on the city's outskirts, building modest, inexpensive track houses. The returning soldiers could get low-cost mortgages, sometimes cheaper than renting an apartment or buying the older row houses. These new homes had more rooms and larger back yards; the lawnmower was now necessary. The baby boom started In 1946, and in the 1950s, around 4 million babies were born. There were nearly 77 million "baby boomers." A new opportunity for people to have larger homes, no more crowded bedrooms, and live in the country. In this new environment, their dreams came true, an exciting new world for some. Factories and businesses started to look at new opportunities. There were still buses, streetcars, and trains. More people were owners of cars, and new modern highways were being built, which allowed people to move around quickly and out of the city. They could now rely on public and private transportation instead of walking to their jobs. Also, the demise of the traditional row house and the Neighborhood structure changed due to the mass exodus in the early '60s. It started with the up and coming, hard-working low and middle class; they wanted something different for their new world, things were changing, and the time was moving on to the future. The younger newly employed with more education than their parents had the prospect of a steady job outside the city. Moving to the Suburbs was the new answer to every question about not staying in the city. More prominent was better; according to some people, the builders profited greatly by selling something fresh and green instead of pavements (sidewalks). The next hit, the closing of factories and moving to the suburbs, changed the ambiance of the city also. Now without employment, the city's decay was evident, and the people could feel and see the coming changes, and they worked hard to accomplish their plan of moving out of their city. These reasons started a landslide that the city and the individual neighborhoods would lose. The vultures told their crime stories, and the end was near philosophy. Investors, we called them blockbusters. It was the way this happened that was heartless; the investors were capitalizing on significantly older populations and unemployed people, fears of a worsening neighborhood thru scare tactics, and they fell for the sales pitch. Some of the older neighbors moved in with their children. Some of the original owners were dying off, which opened the door for the predators. The investors would stroll around the neighborhood, knock on their doors, and ask if anyone wanted to sell their homes. The premise was that if they did not sell soon, their home would be worthless. The investors would buy very low, some houses for under two thousand dollars, and went from individual ownership to rentals, enriching their pockets. No proprietorship put a heavyweight on the old neighborhood. Investors knew that the people had fears of the unknown. What was coming was the end of the Neighborhood as we knew it. Those left behind were the lower-waged working class, the poor, older residents, who could not move, and people who did not want to believe . In the 1950s and 1960s, some old row houses demolished and replaced with so-called apartments; we called them project housing (Public Housing). One large complex was on Fayette Street; this was a big mistake. On paper, the plan looked good, modern high rises, piling more people into smaller spaces for housing Baltimore's population. The buildings were to become the home for the people left behind and the new ones coming, many of who did not have a city living experience. Not the correct way to solve these types of problems. The familiar neighborhood places of business were leaving as fast as the people; the suburbs looked promising. The city demolished the high rises (Projects) in less than 40 years after becoming the city's roughest and most dangerous sections. It was nothing like the row house neighborhood, no community; no one owned their place anymore; the area's pride disappeared. I guess the Department of

Housing and Community Development forgot about the Individual, and now they were back into the high-rise mentality. Not an easy problem to solve; it requires lots of planning and understanding of people. Poor, crowded neighborhoods can be a problem for various reasons, but to pile up and continue to pile up does not make sense. The foresight of all those people who fled the city was correct in their assumption. The change did not envelope the entire city, but the difference was there. Back in the 1800s, they knew the answer. Now in this modern time, it is forgotten. One of the classes in schools should be pride in your Neighborhood. Wonder if 100 years from now, they will be building real row houses again, don't need large houses, making them affordable, the ones the working class could afford, be awarded for their hard work and could say this is their home and their front door and maybe if they are lucky front marble steps and a rose bush, great. Imagine a local large business /factory located near the Neighborhood to hire local people. Maybe a fantasy, but the future is unknown. We know that ownership and pride are equally beneficial for all. I still believe that Baltimore will come back in some ways it already has. But still has a long way to go and will rise to tomorrow's new challenges and maybe develop into an old neighborhood mentality, with most jobs in the city. Is that too much of a goal?

PHOTO COURTESY OF CHARLES ALT

So sits the little house
A gem in someone's eyes
The memories to be forgotten
As a lifetime goes by
To see the passing of the days
The hand of despair is clear
Those who are gone cared
Time has taken its due course
The decay has had its way
Just a glance, we can see
A gem in someone's eyes
written: October 2008 Author: Janet Divel nee Vanik

The one-time resident and a friend took this photo of the house where he grew up during the 1950s/1960s. At the 19th block of North Bradford Street. At that time, it was red brick. This photo gives an example of the different styles of form stone that covered the original brick.

Chapter Two

THE BALTIMORE CONNECTION

Ancestry
      Past, Present, Future
            Birth, Family, Genetic
                Feelings, Senses, Intelligence
                      Resemblances, Connection, Belonging
                          Hours, Days, Weeks
                              Months, Years, Generations
                Ancestors
Written by Janet Divel nee Vanik

My connection to Baltimore started when the Vanik and the Koerner families descended on our shores as immigrants migrating from Germany and Czechoslovakia in the 1980s. This true story about how they created a world that helped form the working class continued their dream. Mine and many other families shaped America and the little city of Baltimore, Maryland. This part of history is put aside and forgotten. Is there any class in school that talks about our immigrant families and what they accomplished thru pure determination? Willpower and purpose are the keywords here. Life was not easy; then, they worked hard and did not expect any free help for themselves and their family. They had to make it happen; if not, fail. Their dreams made our country great. It's not about our wealthy corporations; this was the individuals with small businesses, bruised knuckles, and big imaginations. Salaries were low, and many immigrants were servants and farmworkers unless they had a trade. They had no health care, no Government help; some came over and slept on park benches till they could get a job or two and save for a place to live. During the 1600 and 1700, many immigrants paid for their passage by being indentured servants. They were bound out for years and released after they paid their debt.

In the earlier days, passengers who could not pay for their passages were auctioned and would become indentured servants for a specified time to the successful bidder. After the Revolutionary War, that changed. Between 1820 and 1989, almost 2 million immigrants came to Baltimore, and almost everyone living in the United States today is the descendant of someone who came to this country from somewhere else. Before 1850 the Point of Entry was Fell's Point, Baltimore's first port. Due to a large number of immigrants, Locust Point, next to Fort McHenry, became the new unloading area. On one ticket, immigrants could get a Steamship across the Atlantic Ocean and then travel by railroad to their journey's end. Baltimore was becoming a city of neighborhoods, nativism, and different cultures were working and settling in Little Italy, Canton and Highlandtown. The immigrants who passed through Baltimore to the Midwest and the Great Plains states also rode on the B&O's trains. In 1868, the B & O Railroad partnered with the North German Lloyd (Norddeutscher Lloyd), a steamship line based in Bremen, Germany, Europe's nucleus importation of tobacco. In 1867 immigrants could purchase a single ticket that included both passages on a steamship from Bremen to Baltimore and rail transport to their destination in the central part of the United States. To control the advent of thousands of immigrants, the B&O Railroad built larger immigration passenger cars and an immigration arrival center on piers 8 and 9 in Locust Point; this was replaced with a larger facility in 1904. The cost of a steamship journey costs about $16.00, or in today's math $352.00. $16.00 was a lot of money those days; most immigrants saved for years to make this trip. The immigrant's voyage to America took on an average of two weeks. There were deplorable conditions. A vast open space below the deck was poorly ventilated, crowded, and dirty. They were at constant risk of various illnesses, such as trachoma, a contagious eye disease. Large amounts of people packed tightly together, and bundles of baggage were everywhere on the deck; at that time, they were used as seats and, more likely, their beds. The sounds of men, women, babies, and the children moving around with the constant sounds of several different languages, ship noises, and the anticipation of arriving in port with the concept that if you worked hard, there were jobs to be had with a new start a home, family, and freedom. Imagine those moments. After the ships pulled into Locust Point with the Immigrants, the second half of the journey began. They were looking forward to seeing the American flag as they entered the Baltimore harbor. When arriving at the port, they had a complete physical; if there were any illnesses, they were deported. The second step was an interview by a government agent who counted and reported how much money they brought. Then the baggage was weighed and inspected. I can't imagine what they were thinking, wondering what would happen to them in this strange new place. At the same time, feeling sorrow for what and who they left behind in their homeland. Many of the immigrants came alone to this new land. The lucky ones would have family or friends waiting for them on the pier or destination. Even though many people were going thru this process, there was a silence that seemed strange. No yelling out familiar names or cries. They must have felt insecure, scared, and tired, at the same time feeling full of life and promise.

PHOTO COURTESY OF MARYLAND HISTORICAL SOCIETY

Locust Point receiving docks

Nothing fancy at their arrival; they all have that same weary look. With life processions in Sacks, boxes wrapped packages, and old suitcases 1904-1910.

Immigrant officials put the immigrants in separated into pens. Different ones depending on their destination. Usually waiting for the trains to leave or hopefully have someone they knew meeting them there. During the In the 1890s, there were over 300 sweatshops in Baltimore city, many providing sewing jobs for Immigrants working in the garment industry. Most of the workers toiling in these squalid sweatshops were Bohemian, Italian, Irish, German, Lithuanian, and Russian-Jewish immigrants. Around half of the garment workers were women and girls, many in their early teens and younger.

PHOTO COURTESY OF THE MARYLAND HISTORICAL SOCIETY

The Sonneborn Sewing Factory at Pratt and Paca Street

No coffee breaks those days and no sewing machines, all done by hand.Child labor occurred from the late 1800s thru the 1930s; in 1909, children as young as four years of age worked in meatpacking plants. Like many coastal cities had children shucking oysters, they were expected to work well before dawn and stay till after sunset. I can't imagine the injuries they sustained from the oyster shucker knife. The plight of the poor immigrants of the time. This eight-year-old girl is shucking oysters on the docks for an unidentified cannery in America. Her expression tells the story. Theyear 1912. Lewis Hines took original photos.

COURTESY OF ALAMY

In Baltimore harbor, the oyster boats called (Luggers) would unload their day's catch on the docks down by Pratt Street. The language was a significant barrier, but they all wanted to learn their new American language and imagine people working for the same resolve. Wow, what a great idea! In the early 1900s, there was an Americanization Movement; the immigrants had to assimilate into American society by hurriedly learning the language quickly. Most people do not know what these people sacrificed until we hear the stories. What would it be like to say hi, see their faces, and listen to their voices? What were their personalities and their thoughts? Those that made it possible for us to be here were not always due to planning; sometimes, it was just pure luck that they somehow survived. We should all take note of the past and appreciate their firmness of mind to keep moving forward. The ancestors also knew this from the very beginning. Even though the world is a much different place today, there is something inside us that should stay the same, knowledge of the past and something they call humanity. An ideal of human behavior, tolerance, sympathy, and mostly understanding it's not Utopia. But with some soul history (the past), it might help us be more utopian and find (the Inner Compass). Nostalgia takes us to a place – and the desire to go there again. A place we do not want to go to again would be the historical writings and photos from the works of Photojournalism Jacob Rilis of the mostly European immigrants who lived during the 1880s in the slums of New York City. Titled: How the other half lives. A masterpiece of actual history.

A large portion of the immigrants like the Czechoslovakians (Bohemians) and the Germans came between 1870 and 1890. They came here to escape war, poverty, famine, lack of religious freedom, economic decline, and in some cases, dictatorships. They were against autocracies and did not want to serve in their military. They wanted democracy and to be Free Thinkers. The most significant wave of Czech immigrants occurred from the late 1800s through the early 1900s. Enough Czechs had immigrated by 1860; they created a small colony. The developing community was thriving; by the 1870s, this area, known then as Little Bohemia Village. It continued to grow throughout the 1880s and 1890s. Bohemian immigrants built the homes in that area, most notably the architect Frank Novak (1877-1945).

Many immigrants who settled here worked as weavers and tailors or in market stalls. With further construction in Little Bohemia, the Czech community continued to grow. In 1927 the building was finished in Little Bohemia. As the Czechs began to move into Patterson Park and become an essential component of the neighborhood growth. The Czechoslovakian Society of America founded a duckpin bowling league in 1946. Many of the members were Czech-American soldiers returning from World War 11. Czech-Americans and Slovak-Americans in Baltimore during WWII were strongly opposed to Adolph Hitler and their occupation of Czechoslovakia. After the war, the Czech and Slovaks concentrated in the Collington Avenue area began to move out of the Neighborhood and dispersed widely across Baltimore city.

The mainstream banks during the 1800s and early 1900s would ignore or turn away customers who were of eastern, southern European immigrants, Czechs, and other non-WASP. The immigrants established their banking institutions to serve the specific needs of their communities. The banks had hours and customs that seemed less alien to immigrants and often had translators on staff. Discrimination against Czechs and other immigrants persisted in banking as late as the 1930s and 1940s. It was not uncommon for Slavic Catholics such as Czechs and Poles to be called ethnic and religious slurs such as "bohunks" and "fish-eaters" Slavs were often stereotyped as stupid and superstitious. White Protestants coined "fish eater" to refer to Catholic immigrants because they did not eat meat on Fridays. Discrimination is not a new phenomenon.

The Vanik family, on my paternal side, were Bohemians who came over with a total of 6 individuals, five children, and their Mother, Barbora Vanik nee Stolba. Barbora's husband, Matej Vanik, the father of the children, died before the journey. The family came over at different times, originally consisting of ten children, five died in Bohemia from the whooping cough epidemic in the 1860s, and they were all under the age of two.

On May 16, 1890, the ship SS Karlsruhe arrived in the port of Baltimore. Three of the passengers were Barbora Vanik, my Great-Grand Mother, age 49; Marie, her daughter, age 9; and Vaclav, her son, age 13. Names listed on the ship manifest say the word Wenzel instead of Vaclav. Wenzel is the German equivalent of Vaclav.

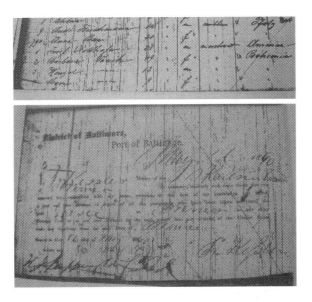

During that time, people living in that part of Europe were under Germanic –Austrian rule. Their official papers were in Czech and German. The embarkation was from Bremen, located in north-eastern Germany. Bremen was a federal state of the new German empire in 1871. The seaport in present-day called Bremerhaven.

During the Historical Czech emigration to America in the late 1800s, some immigrants did not have what is now called a passport. They had to fill out and sign a (Domovsky list) in place of that. It was evidence of residence and occupation with supporting documents and references.

Applicants had to sign that they would waive their residence right to live in the village they were leaving. If not, the town could be liable for the return cost. If the new country refused emigration.

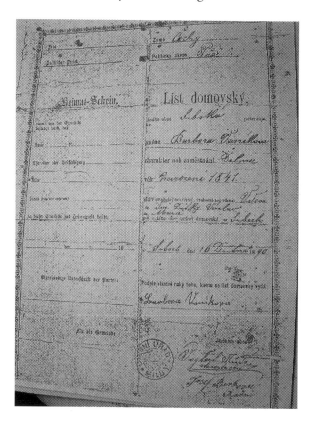

The List Domovsky: German and Czechoslovakian language. A homeland certificate for Barbora Vanik needed this to leave the Austrian Hungarian Empire.

Srbska: She was living in Srby, a village outside Vrcen near Nepomuk
Jmeno: Her name
Delnice: She was of good character
Vidova: She was a widower, with two children, Vaclav and Marie, on this voyage
1890: The year of immigration

Her signature is Barbora Vanikova. Ova or Ovich is an indication of the father's last name.

Barbora Vanik (seated) wearing a babushka scarf worn by peasant women (right to the left) daughter Marie son, Frank Vanik (Frantisek), immigrated here in 1889 at age 20, possible wife of Frank. The year 1895-1900. The Hebbel Photo Studio at 409 N. Gay Street

The Vanik Immigrants

The death rate of children in those days was horrendous. Ten children born and five under the age of two never made it to America. 1900 census shows the Vanik's lived on 369 North Washington Street in Baltimore, Maryland. John Vanik, Sr. According to family history, he was a butcher by trade; in those days, some boys who came over as immigrants already had a career by the time they were twelve years old. The family taught the trades to the young boys. Very important, especially moving to the new homeland, they could contribute to America and support themselves. The story is that when John Vanik Sr. arrived at the Port of Baltimore, he wanted to live in Texas, but he did not have enough money to buy the ticket, so he stayed in Baltimore. He heard that Texas was the biggest beef state, and his skills could get him a job. He brought his butcher knives with him from Bohemia. He also played the accordion and was called the accordion king of northeast Baltimore.

John's children, William and Edward, along with John Jr., were butchers also. They worked at the butcher stall in the Broadway Market in Baltimore City. John Vanik Sr. opened a grocery/meat store at their home on 847 North Montford Avenue, later in 1920, at North Eager Street. John's wife, Frances Vanik Coufal, also worked in the store. During this period, rowhouses were the locations for the local store. It was where families lived; the house, the business, and entrances were either in the front of the house or the side door. Frances had 13 children; four died, ages one year to 6 years old. Imagine raising an average of 10 children and still working every day in a store. These people had the heart and soul and believed that hard work was what you had to do for acceptance in this new country. They had pride in living in this country, now their country. Something that is forgotten or just assumed today is how it's always been.

This picture tells a great story, lots to see. In this photo is my Grandfather, a young John Vanik Jr., third on the left with a white apron and a cigar in his mouth, at his Dad's meat stall at the Belair Market, Forrester And Orleans Street, the early 1900s. The light fixtures look like gas lights, and I can barely see John's letters on top of the photo. I love the character on the left. The butchers laid out beef and pork on the counter. The lady's fancy outfit with a fashionable hat should date this photo.

There was no refrigeration in those days. The ladies would be there daily to get fresh meat and produce. Iceboxes were the freezer of the past. The iceman would deliver a large cube of ice to your home, put it in the icebox, and that was before refrigeration. The old market is gone. Another landmark is gone.

John Vanik Sr.'s brother Frank Vanik was born in 1869 in Srby, West Bohemia, Czech Republic. At the age of eleven, he worked as a blacksmith since twelve and immigrated to Baltimore when he was twenty in 1889, one year before his mother. He was the first of the family to come to America. His family lived at 2438 East Eager Street.

He worked in a Bohemian community located just north of the newly opened hospital Johns Hopkins. The blacksmith at that time saw less and less work and fewer horses; automobiles replaced the horses. So these hard-working immigrants made a change. Many blacksmiths like Frank had to use different tools. The world was moving on. He wanted to keep up and feed his family. He was a blacksmith, a shipyard worker, and later an auto mechanic. At sixty, in the 1930 census, he was still working as a blacksmith and an auto repair shop. Frank and his wife, Frances Vanik nee Kudrna, had 13 Children and twelve survived adulthood.

Frances Vanik nee Kudrna Frank Vanik's wife

In 2015, The city demolished the old home and neighborhood at 2438 East Eager Street. This picture portrays the remaining walls of that house. What a strange, sad beauty.

2438 East Eager Street

Sacrifices continued in the lives of our new citizens, War came, and the young men wanted to fight for their country, the country that gave their parents a new life. Sargent Frank T. Vanik was born in 1893, and Corporal Rudolph Vanik, born in 1897, was ready to serve. I wanted to linger here in this time of history with a bit of extra caring. The heartache that war brings, no matter when it accrues, is still disastrous. The families were torn apart, Not hearing from their children for months, not knowing where they were. In World War 1, two of Frank's sons went to war. One came home, Sgt. Frank T. Vanik did not, a casualty at age 24 in Verdum, Meuse, France, on October 10, 1918.

Frank T. Vanik and his brother Rudolph Vanik
Newspaper article 1918

A two-page letter written by Frank to his sister Agnes Vanik:

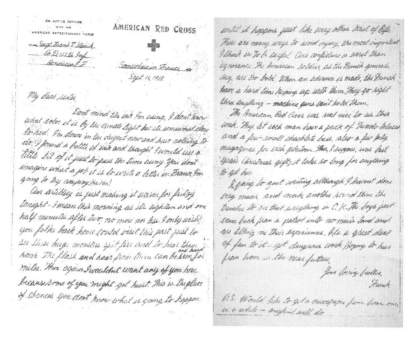

On Sept. 16, 1918, Frank wrote his sister from somewhere in France. Killed on October 10, 1918, less then a month after, he wrote this letter.

The obituary written by the family is heartbreaking and striking words.

VANIK.—In sad but loving remembrance of our dear son and brother, SERGT. FRANK T. VANIK, Company D, One Hundred and Fifteenth Infantry, who was killed in action October 10, 1918.

We do not know the pain he bore,
We did not see him die;
We only know he passed away
And could not say good-by.

Firm as the firmest, where duty led,
He hurried without a falter;
Bold as the boldest, he fought and bled,
And the day was won, but the field was red,
And the blood of his fresh young heart was shed
On his country's hallowed altar.

Our thoughts today are over the sea;
We picture a rough, wooden cross
O'er the grave of a son and brother
None but God can know our loss.

A happy home we once enjoyed;
How sweet the memory still,
But death has left a vacant chair
This world can never fill.
BY HIS MOTHER, FATHER, SISTERS AND BROTHERS.

October 10, Two original wording from death notices written thru the years by the family.

Deep in our hearts lies a picture of a loved one laid to rest, a memory frame we shall keep because he was one of the best by his loving mother, father, sisters, and brothers.

What we give to clasp his hand, his happy face to see, hear his voice, and see his smile means so much to us all. Gone is the face we loved so dear, silent the voice we loved to hear; Upright and just in all his ways, Honest and faithful to the end of his days, by his loving mother, father, sisters, and brothers.

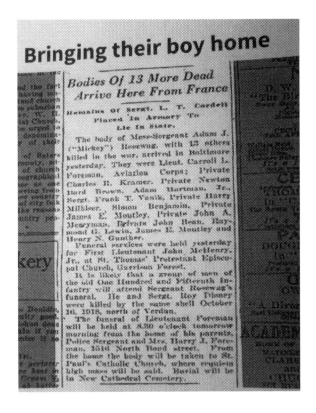

I hope that wars will someday be nonexistent. But unfortunately, we lose our best, yet the monstrous beast continues. I felt compelled to tell this story; it was the right thing to do with this article in the newspaper dated September 23, 1921. Frank T Vanik died on October 10, 1918. There was a three-year wait for the family to recover the remains. That could be the reason for the yearly remembrance in the newspaper until he came home.

Another brother of John Vanik Sr. was Valcav Vanik, who was born in 1877 in Nepomuk, West Bohemia, In the Czech Republic, he came to America with his mother and sister when he was 13; he was a tailor and worked in a clothing factory. He had five children. He was a member of the Sokol movement. Czech immigrants initially brought Sokol to Baltimore in 1872 to maintain a sense of community in a new country. East Baltimore was a center for the Czech-speaking people, known as Little Bohemia. The Sokol movement (Czech word meaning Falcon) is an all gymnastic organization first founded in Prague in the Czech region of Austria -Hungary in 1862 – by Miroslav Tyrs and Jundrich Fugner. Based on the principle of a "Strong mind in a sound body," Providing a forum for spreading mass-based nationalist ideologies.

Valcav Vanik 1910-1920. Vaclav Vanik died in 1935 at the age of 58. He and his wife Marie Vanik nee Kroutil, buried at the Bohemian National Cemetery in Baltimore, Maryland, is in the National Registry as a historical place.

Before Valcav died, his daughter said that he said goodbye to every animal and tree in his place. He was a Freethinker and perhaps more.

Valcav's later years with family

Are family members still putting flowers on this gravestone? The faces on the tombstone have been vandalized thru the years. I took this photo on our visit to the graveyard in 2017. The cemetery is located in an area of decay. A small cemetery, but still hallow ground. One of the last members of the Senior Vanik immigrants were John Vanik Sr.'s Sister, Agnes Vanik, born in 1874 in Srby, Czech Republic. She immigrated here in 1890 at the age of fifteen. She married Tomas Slechta; they had 11 children in eighteen years of marriage. She was married at the age of sixteen in 1891 at St. Wenceslaus Church. I wonder if this could be one of those arranged marriages for the price of the passage? Standard practice for the time. Immigrants that did not have money for that ticket to America promised marriage, servants, farm help, or other arrangements. She died at the age of 64.

Marie (Mary) came over to America with her mother, Barbora Vanik, at nine. She was born in the year of 1879. Pretty in pink certainly fits this picture of Marie. In family comments, she leads the promenade dancing and has a medal on her dress, stating her status. Not sure what that is, but I wager it was a big deal those days.

After Great Aunt Marie married, they lived at 508 North Milton Avenue. The photo next to Marie's is her husband, Peter Charles Nelson. In the later years, her mother, Barbora Vanik, my Great-Grandmother, lived there also. Unknown to me, they lived around the corner where I grew up, only at a different time.

The sturdy, proud and beautiful Bohemians

Katherine Schlecta/
Slechta and Marie 1895

Helen and Walter Gribbon 1920s
Daughter of Agnes Slechta nee Vanik

Helen Slechta

John Vanik Sr, Frances, his wife, and their grown children
Left to right: Charles F., William, James F., John Jr., Edward, Anna, and Amelia
John Vanik Sr. Great-Grandfather sitting, Born 1861 Died September 1936
John Vanik, Jr. Grandfather standing Born 1889 Died July 1966

John Vanik Jr. as a young man lived near St. Wenceslaus Church on Ashland Avenue in Baltimore, Maryland. It was a couple of blocks from the Stecher family's home, his future wife, which was on the corner of Ashland and Collington Avenue right across from St. Wenceslaus Church; feeling sentimental about that because after attending St. Wenceslaus Church and school, I never knew my maternal Grandmother's childhood home was right there. I passed by every day going to school and never knew. Located on Collington Avenue and Madison Street. The house is no longer there. The whole area transformed with the razing of that Neighborhood. The church is still there with minimal services.

When she was nineteen, John Vanik Jr. married Clara Stecher on January 19, 1913. They wed at St. Wenceslaus Church; it was a horse and carriage wedding. Clara made her wedding dress. She played the piano and violin and raised seven children with no running water or electricity. Her Grandfather played the tuba in the John Phillip Sousa Brass Band; his pay was so low that he had to work also as a bricklayer paving the street of East Baltimore.

Wedding Picture John Jr. Vanik and Clara Stecher January 19, 1913; in this picture, both were smiling usually those days, they all had grim faces. Happy Day. I see my brother's eyes in my Grandfather's eyes.

Clara, the Grandmother in the family, was an exciting and personable person; I met her several times as a child. She never wore glasses. She was a small, built person with sad eyes.

Anton Stecker, Clara's father, played the violin and piano at St. Wenceslaus Church and taught Clara how to play the piano and violin. She played her first song when she was five years old at St. Wenceslaus Church. The Stecker family emigrated from Moravia in Czechoslovakia in1885. Anton was nine years old. Anton was a coat maker, and his mother, Frances, was listed as a milliner. The milliner's store was on 901 North Collington Avenue at their home. Clara had 11 siblings born in America. Clara, at age nine, was a very busy little girl. She would bring suits that her mother and father made and bring them down to the Kites Sewing factory to sell. At eight, Clara worked at the Pratt Street docks and shuck oysters.

The oyster boats would come in and dump the oysters into sheds. Czechoslovakian, Polish and Italian Children of all ages would sit on peach baskets, be given an oyster knife, and work all day. We must consider how hard their young lives were. It was all a matter of course for them.

When Clara was 80 years old, she was still playing the piano. She played Happy Birthday to her 60-year-old daughter Frances. Clara died on April 24, 1986, at the age of 93. How did they live so long when you had a hard life?. Maybe It made them reliable and willing to take life how it came. It's the old Iron Will concept (Never give up).

Picture of John Vanik Jr. with a nice side of pork, enjoying his cigar, and Clara at their home on 4200 block of Necker Avenue in Perry Hall in 1934.

Necker Avenue: John and Clara with children, grandchildren, and in 1943 several in uniform. Every family has its characters. Check out the guy in the suit with the hat.

The Vanik house was built-in 1840. The history of that house was irreplaceable. Gerard Vanik, son of John Vanik, spoke in a newspaper article for The Times on March 10, 1988, told the story of how his father bought the house from the Otto family. John later added a pantry, a bathroom, a third bedroom, and some porches to the original structure. The nineteenth-century beams were still in the basement. When the seven Vanik children were small, there was no running water or electricity. There is a filmed record of this little house. A movie company filmed the Blood Massacre, which took place in the house where Gerard had a small part as a video store customer. In October 1987. The interior and the outside canning shed and various parts of the yard are in the film. It's a lasting record, but not sure how the old folks would have liked that movie title. In 1993 the house was demolished for new housing development. it was on six acres. A change came.

This house was a place in my memories of childhood, and I still remember that squeaky wooden porch, the screen door banging closed, high grass, dirt paths, piano in the front room, smells of meat cooking (sausages), sounds of a family and seeing Grandmother Clara's smile. I loved it, wishing I had a large family living near. There were few visits, but I can still visualize the moments. The discovery of the first lighting bug was there to a little city girl; they were wondrous small light bulbs in the air. This page ends my Vanik immigrant family's story. I know that recollections disappear with time, but a book can collect remembrances from the end of an era.

The Vanik family home on Necker Avenue 1940s

German immigrants began to settle along the Chesapeake Bay by 1723, living in the area that became Baltimore in 1729. Following the War of 1812 in North America, a wave of German immigrants came from Palatinate, Hesse, Bavaria, and Bohemia. Many fled from Germany between 1812- 1814, the last of the French Revolutionary Wars and the Napoleonic Wars, to avoid military recruitment into the Royal Prussian Army. The port of Baltimore developed as a gateway for immigrants during the 1820s. It soon became the second-largest gateway to America after New York City, especially at the terminals of the Baltimore and Ohio Railroad on Locust Point, Baltimore, which agreed with the Norddeutscher Lloyd. This German steamship line brought tobacco and German immigrants to the port of Baltimore from Bremen, Germany. German immigrants disembarked from the steamships at B&O's pier, located in Locust Point. The population continued to surge after the Civil War. By 1850, 20,000 German-born people lived in the city. Between 1820 and 1860, Germans were the largest group of immigrants in Baltimore. This wave of immigrants created numerously German institutions, including banks, retail businesses, insurance companies, newspapers, German churches, and schools. By the time of the American Civil War, there were 32,613 German-born residents of Baltimore, not counting their American-born descendants. Many Germans immigrants were political and social liberals and freethinkers who would become politically active.

PHOTO COURTESY OF THE MARYLAND HISTORICAL SOCIETY

Newly built homes in the Camden area, the year 1905, perfect.

My Maternal side family, proud and robust German immigrants, is who I grew up with in East Baltimore City (formally known as Little Bohemia); then became Highlandtown, at least that is what we grew up knowing and that took root. My Mother Madeline Vanik, and her three children moved into our Grandparents' house. Elizabeth Koerner, in 1943 at 408 North Port Street, a tiny place, and sharing beds was not unusual those days. There was a newborn, a two and a 4-year-old, plus three adults. For a 14-foot wide house, that was a full house, but I never noticed.

This segment is about George and Elizabeth Koerner, my Grandparents on my maternal side. The Koerner name came from Bavaria (Germany). According to the passenger list, my Great Grandfather George M. Koerner was my first ancestor to arrive in America. He came alone on the ship Capella and arrived at Baltimore Port from Baden, Germany, in September 1867. He was 24 years old, and his occupation was a tailor. He was born on July 6, 1842. His parents were Nic Batz and Margaret. George married a year later to Anna Marie Kuhn, age 18. Her parents' names were Andreas and Walburga Kuhn from Germany. It said that Anna had a mean disposition, smoked cigars, and was artistic. She wore her hair in a knot. George was knowledgeable and a male chauvinist. They were married in 1868 at St. Michaels Church on Wolf Street in Baltimore. I think this was a planned marriage, and Anna's family paid for George M. Koerner's passage to America. They lived at 19 North Wolf Street in 1899 and on Chapel Street in 1910. At her passing, she lived at 401 North Robinson Street. They had nine children; six survived. Sure glad that George survived; it's a good thing to have your ancestor stay alive. George Joseph Koerner, my maternal Grandfather, was born in May 27, 1871.

In his younger years, he was on his way to becoming a teaching brother. It was a Roman Catholic Marian society, a congregation of brothers and priests. They believed that the best ways to live a spiritual life were to share their faith with others, work with the poor, and educate and nourish the mind, the body, and the soul.

It was intense formation processes that led them to examine themselves and their spirituality. The first step to becoming a Marianists is to be a Contact. Contacts learn about the religious institute and themselves through retreats and through the guidance of Marianists, whom they would contact regularly. The next step is the Aspirancy, a 10-month journey of living with a Marianists community and following its daily practices. Each aspirant works in a ministry to further their understanding of spirituality and faith. At the end of this period, one enters the Novitiate, which is 20 months divided over two years.

During that time, the novice learns about the institute and spends time deeply discerning his call to the institute. At the end of the Novitiate, the novice professes Temporary Vows. He must annually renew the vow for at least three years. At the end of that time, the brother can decide to enter into a Perpetual Profession, the brother will profess the vows of poverty, chastity, obedience, and stability. My Grandfather chose not to stay. While searching with my uncle through his old photos and Paperwork, we found a letter to my grandfather's mother. Written that she should be ashamed of her son and disown him. I never got to finish reading it, my uncle asked for it, and it disappeared. My uncle felt ashamed, still from the old school, and religion was a strong connection. Those days it was shameful if you turned your back on your faith. However, my great-uncle Andrew became a teaching brother of Mary and taught at the University of Dayton in Ohio. It was an honor for young men to become Brothers, they had a place to live, and many families in those days were impoverished. One way to survive poverty was to tell your son or sons this was their calling. Many young men left home for their religion. They wore itchy wool robes with rope ties around their waist. Not a very comfortable way to live. George made his way back to Baltimore, and on June 1st, at the age of thirty, he got a job at the Benjes Hotel. Wages for July were $9.00. He later earned a clerk job at the Baltimore and Ohio Railroad. On September 3rd, 1901, his salary was $20.00 per month. George boarded at Ackermann's Boarding house, a row house, and paid $14.00 a month. March of 1902, he got his first raise of $2.35 per month. George spent one cent on Lizzie (Elizabeth Barthel) on August 1st, 1902, his salary was $25.00 per month, and he started to live at a boarding house called Thelma's. On Friday, October 24, 1902, he made $30.00 per month. Below are some of Georges treasures:

Homemade small stool 9 inches by 5 inches   *Marching soldiers from a long-ago war*

The lady below is a drawing George Koerner did, date probably early 1900, called "Know all men by these presents." It speaks for itself, but it looks like he never finished with the drawing, and why? It's an incomplete picture

Early 1900's postal scale

This small tin box was George's money box in the early 1900s

Below is the design on the side of the scale

George had four brothers, Conrad, Nicholas, Edward, and Andrew, who was a teaching brother in Ohio.

George is third from the left, cigar in hand. What a gang. Pictures make the people come to life; they existed and were extraordinary second generation.

A popular pastime at 803 Boulton Street backyard is shucking and eating oysters (Koerner brother Nick and Ed)

There was an article in the 1940 B & O Railroad magazine: Who can beat a record like this – George Koerner, Statistical Department, has about completed forty years of service with the company and, in all that time, has not been absent a single day because of illness. What a record. He attributes his excellent health to exercise as he walks to and from work every day. Making a total of sixty blocks – when he was 69 years of age, he was still working. In November 1902, he moved again to North Wolf Street. In 1903 his salary was raised to $40.00 a month. In January 1904, he managed to save and had in the bank $300.00. 1905 his salary was $50.00 a month.

You might be curious about how I knew these acquired facts. Notable my Grandfather left a journal; the start date of this small book was December 1900. It's a Chronicle of time that has gone.

> What sits in this little book?
> It has the words of their lives
> To see the actual writings
> To feel the movement between the pages
> Is there still an aura on this paper?
> I know, do you?
> Written: March 2017 Author: Janet Divel nee Vanik

George Koerner's journal and coin purse Year 1900

Remarkable enough, I can share a piece of my grandparents' life through a small journal's pages.

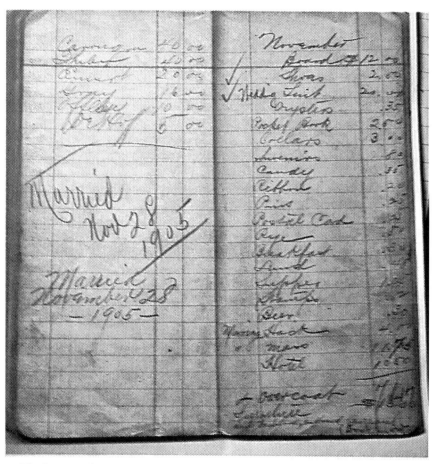

The first page of Journal Year 1900   *1903 Expenses of that era*

Marriage in Baltimore, Maryland Year 1905 George Koerner and Elizabeth Barthel

Honeymoon to New York by train B & O

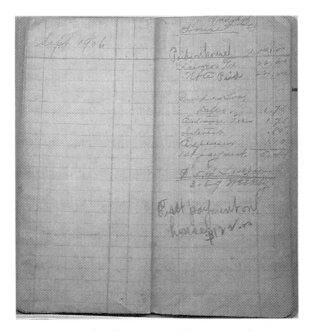

*Regarding the purchase of the home at 408
North Port Street - September 1906*

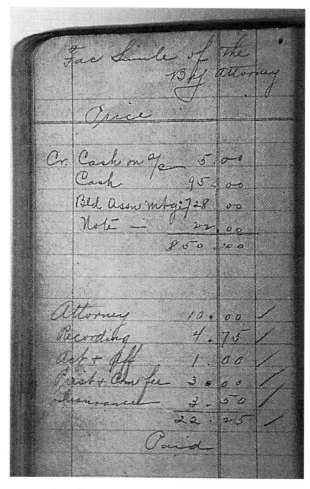

Purchase of home – 408 North Port Street Price $850.00

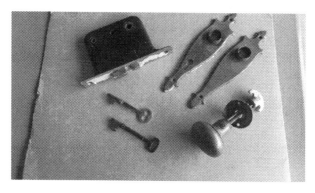

Some of the reminders of the old house

This 19 deep, 30 long, and 16-inch trunk tells a story about coming from the old country and bringing all your belongings in this holder of objects. The chest came from Germany in the late 1800s. It sat in the basement of Port Street for storage. Now that the light is on, it looks worn and still has a forever beauty.

This coat hanger had a place of honor in the hallway by the front door from 1910 to the 1990sOn the right, the shipping label on the back of the mirror, though damaged, we can see it shipped to Mrs. Koerner, my Grandmother. I especially like the Highlandtown wording. I've never seen that on any label before.

In the National Archives, Elizabeth (Lizzie) Barthel, my maternal grandmother, was an indentured servant at a young age. According to family information, she was ten years old when she moved to North Wolf Street, then lived at 2036 Bank Street with the Thill family. The city census stated at age 22, she was listed as a servant and lived there until she was married. It was a typical arrangement in those days. Some had too many children to feed, and arranged marriages were also for a price. Indentured servants, similar to debt bondage, was a contract signed by a person or family, maybe parents, stating working without a salary and housed, clothed, and fed until the repayment for a debt or other. Some indentured servants had their transportation paid to come over to the new country for their services. No walk in the park for poor people who were indentured servants.

It's hard to believe that this was going on not long ago; it's easy to perceive, mainly because that generation struggled. Many immigrant children never had a childhood. But yet, not too many people are familiar with this happening. Elizabeth Barthel's father, Philippa, an immigrant from Germany, was a street cleaner; the story is he died of sunstroke while working. Her mother's name was Eva Dressel. Elizabeth Barthel was indentured until she married George Koerner Jr. She had minimal education and wrote poorly.

She had problems with her feet due to years of wearing shoes too small. Elizabeth was very stern, had blue eyes, and could speak German. She loved sweets, especially donuts and peach cake, and got to see Deborah Lee, in 1958, her great-granddaughter.

Elizabeth (Lizzie), the 1890s/

George Koerner Jr. took a bride and bought a wedding suit for $20.00, a wedding ring for $11.00, and married Elizabeth Barthel in September 1906. They purchased a small row house at 408 North Port Street, Northeast Baltimore. The cost of the house was $850.00. In his ledger, he wrote that after the down payment, he had a loan from the Building and Loan Association of $728.00 and paid $3.69 weekly. Would you believe the lawyer's cost was $10.00? At that time, George worked for the B & O Railroad as a clerk, and in 1906 was paid $50.00 a month salary. Their honeymoon cost $21.15. A train ride to New York City and a hotel room for $10.50. George Koerner was a soft-spoken man who smoked cigars, and, as a small child, I became the recipient of the cigar band ring. He enjoyed a pint of beer now and then. George was a man of many hobbies and interests, loved music, and played a violin and harmonica. He had a stamp and postcard collection and was a lover of animals and plants, a collector, and an artist. We were very young when my Grandfather passed away, but I was left thinking and curious about life. He enjoyed going down to the cellar where he kept his pickled pig's feet and enjoyed a few pig's feet while playing one of his three one-sided records on the old turntable. His favorite, "You're a grand old rag," sounded squeaky like someone very far away singing. He must have loved that song and after all, The lyrics on the next page are from that patriotic song from 1901 thru 1906.

An original record (photo below) with a patent of 1901 and January 1906, written by George M. Cohan, and the solo tenor was Billy Murray. Here are the Lyrics Grand old flag (rag)

There's a feeling that comes a-stealing, and it sets my brain a-reeling
When I'm listening to the music of a military band.
Any tune like "Yankee Doodle" Simply sets me off my noodle,
It's that patriotic, something that no one can understand.
"Way down south, in the land of cotton,"
Melody untiring, Ain't that inspiring?
Hurrah! Hurrah! We'll join the jubilee!
And that's going some, for the Yankees, by gum! Red, white and blue, I am for you!
Honest, you're a grand old flag!
I'm no cranky hanky panky,
I'm dead square, honest Yankee,
And I'm proud of that old flag that flies for uncle Sam.
Though I don't believe in raving ev'ry time I see it waving
There's a chill runs up my back that makes me glad I'm what I am
Here's a land with a million soldiers,
That's if we should need 'em, We'll fight for freedom!
Hurrah! Hurrah! For every Yankee tar and G.A.R. E ev'ry stripe, ev'ry star.

Red, white and blue. Hat's off to you. Honest, you're a grand old flag!
Your're a grand old flag, You're a high flying flag
And forever in peace may you wave.
You're the emblem of the land that I love-the home of the free and the brave.
Ev'ry heart beats true 'neath the Red, White and Blue, where there's never
a boast or brag.
But should auld acquaintance be forgotten, keep youe eye on the grand old flag
The tools used to keep the household going were practical for the time.
Now they would all be a question?

I remember watching my Grandmother Elizabeth darn socks with this.

This twenty-nine-inch contraption is a rug beater

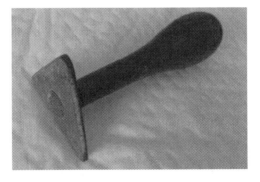

Gadget, I have never been able to figure out what it is?
There was always something special. Elizabeth's Shirley Temple pitcher

Ink and pen sketched by George Koerner, 1906/1910

Only a few things remain from George. What did survive are the most important things. After my Grandfather passing, my Mother, found his ledger dating to 1900. Also, artwork in various forms. It's a fantastic tapestry, how we go thru life not knowing about the people we descended from, things passed on explaining a tradition and who the people were and who you are. It's funny the more that's known about our ancestors, the more we sense ourselves. Their nectar is running thru our veins.

George Koerner as a young man, year about the mid-1890s

After their wedding, George and Elizabeth set up a house. The Port Street property had gas lights and an outhouse at the bottom of the yard near the fence line, probably about 30 feet from home. It was a row house, 14 feet wide. The back yards were as wide as the house, and some people put in small gardens. George planted a dark red rose bush tucked in his three ft. by four ft. area. The story was that he picked up that beauty in an abandoned cemetery. It was his pride and joy. He had a nonstop supply of fertilizer. The hucksters who sold veggies and fruit and some offering services like sharping knives and scissors had largewagons. The power source was the horses leaving presents for all the gardeners in the Neighborhood. There were times when the backyard would have a terrible odor, and George was the cause. George would open the gate and venture into the alley with a shovel in hand; the stuff was still smoking, and into the garden it went. Box turtles would appear in the yard; George would find them near the train tracks. The problem with the turtles, they like to dig and hibernate. All the rest of the yard was concrete, except for the tiny garden, and the turtle would hibernate in the winter, and next spring, it seemed like they disappeared going the wrong way under the concrete, and what a horrible ending for them. Back River is now considered one of the most polluted waters in Baltimore and used to be George's favorite fishing spot. I had no idea how he got there, and he never had a car. He would come home with catfish and eels. He cleaned the eels and catfish down at the bottom of the yard, pulled the skin off with pliers, and then proudly brought than to the kitchen. Yucky, that was dinner.

Elizabeth was very stern. She never showed any affection toward us. I think that is how she, as an indentured child servant, was treated. Being a member of the Jolly Twelve Club seemed to make her happy. Elizabeth is first on the left.

THE YEAR 1948

The club consisted of twelve ladies from the Neighborhood. They loved day trips by bus; one of the spots to visit was Pelz's Shore in Middle River. Now that I am older, I understand the hard life she had as a child and probably never had the opportunity to grow up in a loving family, and her friends were essential.

Photo: 803 Boulton St. Home of Ed Koerner, George's brother, 1917. Sign of the times: straw brooms, chickens, and outhouse covered by an American flag, right in the middle of Baltimore city. Patriotic. The photo includes Grandfather George, Elizabeth, and two children, Mats and Mary. I love this image!

Elizabeth and George Koerner, Year early 1940's and there is that cigar again. I love the hat, gloves, and purse. George and Elizabeth had four live birth children. The first son named George died at the age of nine in

1916. They said he had brain fever, difficulty walking, and weakness in his body. Now we know it was Muscular Dystrophy.

Mary, another daughter, born in 1916, passed at the age of 101 in 2017. She was brilliant and still, when she was 102, gave you a run for your money. The second George Jr. was born in 1921 to 1999. Naming your children after a child that passed away was a common thing. George had many interests and knowledge of different things. When in town, he would come and visit us on Port Street and bring scrap paper for my brothers and me. Paper just for drawing was hard to come by. It was not considered necessary. It was a gift truly appreciated.

This piece of the story is all about Madeline (Mats) Koerner, my Mother. Madeline worked most of her life as a saleslady. Other jobs were cleaning houses. She was a powerful woman and financially raised three children on her own. Magdalene, according to her birth certificate, was born at home at 408 North Port Magdalene, according to her birth certificate, was born at home at 408 North Port street on March 20, 1912. She always insisted her birthday was March 17, which was the date it was celebrated. She fell in love and married Joseph Vanik on June 1st, 1936, at St. Michael's church, South Wolf Street, Baltimore, Md. He bought a row house on Beryl Avenue, East Baltimore.

Joseph Vanik Age 22 , born on Oct 3rd, 1914 and Madeline Koerner
Age 24 , born March 17th, 1912 , were married on June 1, 1936
at St. Michaels Church on 7 South Wolf Street, Baltimore, Maryland.

However, her life changed drastically. Joseph left the family and moved to Florida. On that day, a new baby, Richard, was brought home; Joseph Vanik, our father, left home and never returned to being a father with three children. Because of one parent's digression, we descended into the world of poverty. I can't imagine what Madeline's thoughts were; in those days, the way of thinking was without a man, a woman could not raise children. Joseph Vanik sold the home; oddly enough, she never saw a dime, and now she was homeless with three young children. No child support thru those years. My Grandparents, George and Elizabeth Koerner, came to the rescue; they had that tiny house on Port Street that took Madeline and her little family in. We were now part of the Port Street family, and we could have just as well been separated and put in a state home, which the city was considering. The Children's Welfare Dept. came to the house one day and lined my brothers and me up against the wall, put a paper tag with a number and our names on it, and took our picture; Madeline had one photo for identification for their next surprise visit to our home. Having a disabled child in the mix made the situation more challenging. My oldest brother, Bobby, had Muscular Dystrophy, which is a muscle-wasting disease with a life expectancy of 18 to 19 years of age. Bobby lost his ability to walk at age nine. He was able to attend William's S. Baer School until he could no longer walk. There was no way to get him to the bus. Those days children like him were called crippled, crazy, or something worst. Now there is a different name they have (disabilities). Life was very hard on Bob; his bathroom facilities were in the kitchen; no one could carry him up the stairs when he got older. He spent most of his life in the living room of 408 North Port Street, where he passed away on the couch at nineteen. The day he passed, the Doctor was at the house, and as Bobby was gasping for air, Doc uttered nothing could help him. Just let him be. I looked at that Doctor's face in disbelief. I guess I was expecting something else. I looked down at Bob and ran out the front door, and I ran till I could not run anymore. That was the last time I saw him alive. I finally stopped in front of a church and sat on the steps; after the darkness came, I made my way back home. I was Fourteen years old and confused; how could they let him just die? Bob was gone, his couch was empty, and there was silence for my brother Richard and me. Those days, these things were, I guess, considered the norm, and we must move on. We knew things were going to be different. Watching my brother die is an edged picture in my mind forever. Still, today, I can find that bruise tucked in my heart. Bobby was a brilliant and kind-hearted person: he would have been a good man. Even today, there is no cure for this disease. As time went by, a reckoning was coming. The father who abandoned our family should know what he did to his children and the consequences of his actions. One evening in 1995, after losing my second and younger brother, and my father was still alive, it was time. A letter was written, releasing me from the burden, and it worked; it was for all our family members. Our intuition alone taught us how to deal with life and gave us a new compass for the future.

Even with a significant disadvantage, Madeline showed them. Thanks to my mother, working in a department store as a saleswoman. Many nights she came home, her feet swollen from standing all day. She was subjected to an armed robbery at the pet department of Hecht May Co., several muggings, but still never wavered. She also worked as a house cleaner for other people's homes and still had that determination to keep the family together. This story was the beginning of my little Port Street family and the Baltimore connection for the rest of my life. She is my brave and soulful ancestor. The fact that she never complained is remarkable. Madeline passed at the age of 86 in 1997.

Call them souvenirs, remembrance, keepsakes; can you feel them?

Love you, Mom

Janet, Richard, Bobby, and Mom, Easter, the year 1948, 408 North Port Street backyard

Ancestry is a remarkable thing that is physically and mentally in our bodies and soul. We should always consider how far we have come. After all, we are a montage of all the faces and souls before us.

Chapter Three

THE NEIGHBORHOOD: SOUNDS, SMELLS, SIGHT, AND PEOPLE

PHOTO COURTESY OF AAUBREY BODINE

What is a Neighborhood: The dictionary says it means friendly relations,neighbors,neighborliness, the state or quality of being neighbors, a community district, or area, esp. about some characteristic or point of reference, the people living near one other; community. I felt that the word Neighborhood had a story to be told. When this undertaking started, I expected to do a two-page summary of this topic. But, one night, sitting down by the computer, the shedding of my thoughts ran enthusiastically with memories of the people and growing up in Highlandtown. In a neighborhood located in East Baltimore city thru the 40s, 50s, and 60s, I soon realized that this was more than two pages. It became more than a couple of pages or a small book. It emerged as a constant flow of old recollections, thoughts, and visuals that would not stop. Our experiences, including the history of family, environment, and people we have met along the way. Became our philosophy and remembrances that we keep? I feel that all together, it's what ignites us. The aspiration to know the past became an eager desire to write a story with the connection of two passions, Ancestry and City, together. I will try to take us down memory lane, and there will be a piece of us reunited. Not knowing where to begin but understanding that we can connect all things, I'm starting and ending with a mixture of sounds, smells, sights, and People.

Janet Divel nee Vanik Memory Lane June 1955

To start our journey, I want to go back to that time. Let's walk out the front door of 408 North Port Street in east Baltimore and step out to the top step. Look down on beautiful clean white polished marble. When the sun would shine at the right angle at a particular time of day, the marble steps sparkled like scattered flakes of diamonds.

There were spic and span pavements (sidewalks) and an uncluttered narrow street, wide enough for a car with a few feet to spare if you looked right or left. Across the street are more row houses. All the houses were in a neat connected row. Some of the houses had the exterior of red brick unpainted with painted white, gray, or green wooden window shutters, great for a rainy day or night. The windows were left open in the warm weather, there was no air-conditioning, and getting that breeze was heaven-sent. You would see a large tree down at the end of the block, which was the only green feature around. At the end of each block, there were cross streets wider than Port Street. There was a constant flow of cars and trucks, adding to the voice of the city neighborhood.

Street view 1969 East Orleans Street and the cross street North Milton Avenue (looking east)

PHOTO COURTESY OF BALTIMORE MUSEUM OF INDUSTRY

I feel like it was yesterday when I would walk down this street. Typical, the street would be busy with traffic looks like a very early Sunday morning. On the left side was the Jenkins produce stand and market where the soft crabs would be on display to buy.

Cleanliness was an essential part of city living: it was a form of gratification for rigid people who worked to get to this point, to buy their own home. The older people used to say cleanliness is next to godliness, along with many other hypotheses. Neighbors would be out front and back with their hoses and brooms, cleaning the street and alleys. Clean windows were also a crucial customary routine. I can remember sitting on the ledge of the upstairs window, feet facing in, holding on, and wiping that glass. The secret was to hold on to the side of the windows with the other hand. Those windows were always spotless. There was a lot of pride in how your street and house looked, not fancy or freshly painted but clean. If you were standing out front in the evening, there was a sound of constant movement. In the summertime, neighbors would be sitting on the cool marble front steps to discuss the latest news and gossip. The sounds of church bells, voices, traffic, chattering city sparrows, with pigeons cooing, add to the outdoor concert. Welcome to old Baltimore. Welcome to Highlandtown. Pronounced "Hilantown"

North Port Street rear yard, the year 1959, when the wooden fences were still there. With a layer of snow.

Back yard beach and pool 406 North Port Street rear yard Year 1960

Our Neighborhood was a mixture of blue-collar, poverty, and low income. Assistance from the city was very sparse, and people were too proud to ask for it. There was a lot of poverty. My brothers and I grew up in this environment, classified as underprivileged children in those days. We were underprivileged but did not know that or even what that meant. Things given were few. At times I would go into a house and notice that the children slept on the floor with a mattress or blankets. How lucky I was to share a bed with my mother. Many details still are vivid in my mind. Missing breakfast or lunch was not unusual for many families. Spaghetti sauce was tomato paste, eating Brussels sprouts for dinner, jelly sandwiches absent of peanut butter, and bologna sandwiches when available. Babies in drawers, used as a crib, and always second-hand clothes. These are all things I have seen and more, but there was the Neighborhood, which kept us all connected, and if anyone needed help, a neighbor would help if they could. Growing up in poverty, we learned early to step up and take care of ourselves. We were all at our best when we had that connection. There were times when a neighbor would give baths to the neighbor's children in need. It was not all about giving money; no one had any extra. People helping people were all in this together theory. It was even common practice for a neighbor to look out for other neighborhood children and discipline them if they deemed necessary. Living in the Neighborhood at that time was first and second-generation European Immigrants. In old Europe, people (neighbors) felt responsible for protecting the villages. Their mindset was rooted in their memories and traditions. Being in a new strange world, they had to stick together to make it. There is a saying it takes a village to raise a child. In the new world, the village became the Neighborhood.

We need to know the history and culture to understand the dynamics of their way of thinking. Hoping to do that, I saved and wrote thru the years. Was there a thought that I needed this for something, sometime, somewhere, or being a hoarder of memoirs? Well, there is a conclusion. Yes, there is a need for collectors now and in the future for all memories and histories. How will anyone know the neighborhood's past and understand the people? They belonged to the city. It's not all about tearing buildings down and wondering what was there in the years-long gone; it's about the flesh and blood people who lived there that are more important. Their breath is still among us. We all feel nostalgia; it takes us to a place, a place and culture you ache to go to again, and the only way to get there is thru memories. The past and future of Baltimore are the spirit, souls, and story of Baltimoreans That they were there and written about and how wonderful and not so wonderful it was.

Just a thought
Is there a chance we are meant not to wonder?
But to hold together the connection we have.
Separation brings woe, melancholy, and the desire to come together.
How much will we change in the future if we believe the past is obsolete?
Will we lose ourselves?
Maybe, no conscience or identification
Written April 2017 Author: Janet Divel nee Vanik

Backyard view of electric wires, clotheslines, and the neighborhood tree. The year 1980

TV Antennas

The daily breathing of their lives continues thru descriptions. The Bowen family lived two doors down with the backyard pigeon coups and had a coup as big as the yard. The sounds of cooing were all day. Mr. Bowen would release the pigeons every morning, and off they would go flying in a large circle around the block, their wings flapping as they took off. They seemed happy to be free; however, the ladies in the neighborhood were not pleased. Besides the foul smell, the clothes hung out on the line in your backyard, and there was constant complaining about pigeon droppings on the clean clothing. Eventually, the city made it illegal to have pigeon coups due to the rat population. The structures, including the coups and fences, were made of old wood and were declared a nuisance.

Image is not available, but imagine a lady in her city backyard a high wooden fence, hanging clothes on the clotheslines. The story goes like this: Concrete ground with bricks laid on the small patch of dirt to keep unwanted critters out, the wooden clothespins, a used wooden bushel basket now used for a laundry basket, dented metal trashcan, and the clothespin bag around her waist, and of course, the housedress that most women wore those days. The breeze was the dryer. The sounds of traffic, children's echoes, and the sound of sparrows fluttering and flying around looking for crumbs were the entertainment.

Anticipated back in the late '40s, a photographer huckster went door to door and asked if we would like to have a picture taken on a pony.

They had all the gear, hat, scarf, chaps, and the pony. My brother Richard was the lucky one that day; He was so happy. They used him as a sample picture, a good day. The image below is Richard Vanik. Those days the cowboy was what all little boys aspired to be. It was never a girl's thought to have her picture on a cowboy horse. Girls were to be more submissive in their behavior. Poverty brought more problems for the children. Those were not always the good old days.

408 North Port Street Year 1947

Humor man – city or country, 1950 speaks for itself. City living was the existence of a contact with people. It is like a Facebook account; only it was visual and physical; there was interaction. It was an education all in itself everyday. Besides the typical day, there were other distractions. Our Amazon were real people, including the VacumnCleaners salesmen, the Fuller brush salesmen, Encylopedia salesmen, Wear-Ever pots and pans salesmen, and Life Insurance agents, who would come to your home and take your weekly payment. The milkman, screen painters, house painters, iceman deliveries, coal deliveries, and even your mortgage lender would stop by. There were conversations with the street cleaners, garbage men, or just a friendly neighbor. In the mid-fifties, certain streets would have block parties, this concept seems unbelievable, but it did exist. Remembering the 400 blocks of north Bradford street in the early '50s. The street was closed that day; there were saw horses out on the payment with food items. Some of the houses had their door open; anyone could enter, get something to eat from the kitchen table, and leave. An honor system. Basement windows were available, and the neighbors that attended these parties were people who lived on that block and had guests. Everyone pitched in with home-cooked food.

Photo courtesy of A Aubrey Bodine View down Patterson Park
Avenue from Jefferson Street towards Orleans 1945

This church had an actual bell tower and would play a musical bell concert every quarter, half, and hour. I still remember the melody. A higher range Dong Dong Dong Dong, then a lower range Dong 4 times again and the countdown of hours. One chime for one o'clock, etc. We never needed a watch and always knew what time it was. There was no excuse for being late for dinner.

We had our local bookie (bookmaker); she lived up the street. Mrs. H. was a busy lady besides raising six children. Her customers were the trash men, mailmen, locals, and other characters willing to gamble. Mrs. H. had large breasts, and her bra was a filing cabinet for safekeeping of the cash. She was one of the ladies who were always ready to help a neighbor.

My favorite aspect of city living were the alleys. They were a shortcut, great for roller skating, garbage trucks, hucksters, and another depiction of the city.

COURTESY OF AAUBREY BODINE

Poly Street looking toward Monument Street late 1940s

COURTESY OF AAUBREY BODINE

Photo of Durham Street alley between Jefferson Street and Orleans Street in 1945. Despite the poverty in the area, the noticeable thing is the cleanliness of the alleyways.

The Hucksters were our first door-to-door delivery man before Amazon would come down the street or alley with a horse and wagon selling fruits and veggies. Then, the watermelon man yelled "watermelon" on his way down the street or alleyway. He would cut a pyramided slice to test for sweetness. Later during the day, the alley was a busy place again. Another huckster, only this one yelling, "get your scissors and knives sharpened here." There was even a ragman selling rags.

COURTESY OF AAUBREY BODINE YEAR 1945

As the '50s disappeared, so did most of the hucksters. The stable I remember was located on North Bradford Street and East Monument Street and owned by Albert Vetters. Also on that block was a row house, where people made straw brooms. It was over for that way of life when the stables shut down. There was a home delivery service of milk, names such as Green Spring, Sealtest, and Cloverland. A layer of cream sat the top of the milk; shaking it up got that cream mixed in. That service disappeared in the early '50s. It was not unusual to see a group of guys singing Cappella hanging out on the street corners, mainly on Patterson Park Avenue and Madison Street, at P.S. 13 School. They had a lot of space for an audience. That was the time of an awakening baby; the music was Rock and roll, rhythm, blues, Soul, Motown, Elvis, Bill Halley, the comets, and the Platters. Just a tiny part of what was happening. It was time to embrace it, and music became an essential part of our young culture.

As a kid growing up, our favorite thing to do before the teen years was street skating, metal skates with a unique all-purpose key. The clamps on the skate would attach to the side of the shoe. The key was to tighten the grip, remove the metal wheels, and adjust the skates' length for a perfect fit. This key was always put on a string around the neck for easy access.

It was exhilarating to skate down the streets and jump over the curbs. Our braking system was going sideways; no safety issues here. We had complete confidence in those metal wheels. Or did we think we were invincible?

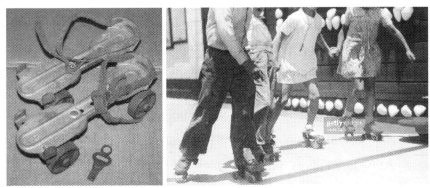

COURTESY OF GETTY PHOTOS

NO FEAR

Indoor skating was another option, and of course, there was a neighborhood skating rink, Skateland, located on 3420 Fleet Street (Highlandtown). Pom Poms and sometimes bells were the fashion style for skates in the 1950s

Several rinks outside our area were New Essex Roller Rink in Essex, Carlins Roller Rink in Carlin's Park located on Druid Hill Drive, Royal Roller Rink in Hagerstown, and Washington Roller Skate Rink at 1103-09 North Washington Street. Most are gone.

The kids could not always pay for entertainment, but that did not stop them from entertaining themselves. Always kept busy; there were, at all times, kids around. We chose to play Hopscotch, usually played with a heel of an old shoe found in the back alley of the shoemaker shop, cut-out dolls, making potholders Jump rope, (double scotch) Mother may I, Redline, and tag. Or we were hanging out on the front steps or by the lamp post, usually the meeting place for just paling around. Counting cars a step activity was one of the games; the game had to be on Orleans Street, where the heavy traffic was, and whoever counted the most out-of-state tags was the winner. Honor system.

Ball and Jacks, to play the game: throw the ball up and see how many jacks could pick up with your one hand and catch the ball. Marbles, card throwing, stickball, and handball ball would use the flat part of the hand to hit the ball against the wall to score and stickball. There is no fancy hardware here. Any game hitting the ball were window breakers.

If boredom set in, then you would try to find something new. Maybe not everyone would agree with me. How about looking for roach eggs, putting them in a jar, and watching them hatch. There was a day when I wondered if I could hatch a chicken egg, I would like to have a baby chick, that was not a good idea, but at the time, it seemed fitting. So I took an egg, wrapped it up in a handkerchief, put it in my mother's dresser drawer, and then forgot about it. There was this horrible stink as time went by, and the dresser drawer was suspect. I held my nose and removed it, but I learned a lesson, and my Mother was very understanding. On rare occasions, there were unusual visitors to the city, and the challenge was to try to catch the occasional grasshopper or lighting bugs. Gee, what did we do without TV?

Other than traffic sounds, in the 1940s, old instrument sounds were available, and mostly polka music originated from Poland. It is a lively dance for couples of three quick steps and a hop. This instrument was the Accordion; it had that soulful cultural sound. There were evenings while walking down the narrow city alleys, the glow from the lights from the windows and hearing that sound have stayed with me. I'm back at that city alley again when an accordion is playing.

They were singing songs in the backyards like Goodnight Irene was popular. Television was a scarcity during the 1940s and '50s. Although television service began in the US on July 2, 1928, the high prices and lack of programs kept people from buying them. In 1947 there were 40 million radios and 44,000 TV sets, mainly in New York. By 1952 1.4 million families had acquired TVs, and by the late '60s and '70s, TV had come into extensive use. We did not have a TV until 1953; there were visits to neighbors to see the Steve Allen Show. Some of the TVs had 6-inch round screens and could receive two channels. Most of the time on the screen was snow, blurry white spots, and a sizzling sound. Not continually living with a TV made people live a different life than today. In the 1960s, strange metal things called an antenna got attached to the roofs. There were bunny ears and a small antenna that would sit on top of the TV and move the ears (rods) to the reception. Another way to get that better picture was to put aluminum foil on the ears. It worked sometimes.

bunny ear

*My brother Bobby a victim of Muscular Dystrophy got his
wish from Tall Cedars Organization, a TV. 1953*

Here is a perfect example of a 1953 TV available with two channels and had to practically sit on top of it to see that fuzzy picture. This TV did not have an antenna on the roof, only bunny ears.

Another essential part of life in the neighborhood was the Provisions, Chow, Grub, and Sustenance. It is all foodstuff. Our food links us to our heritage; it is part of our roots and a topic that excites the various smells' senses. In the neighborhood, food smells were at their peak during the summer. The windows always opened, and a release of familiarity floated out. In the following pages, we will go thru our neighborhood's acquired sense of taste. There were two crab houses less than a block away from Port Street. On the 2400 block of Orleans Street, Patterson Park Avenue,

Milton Avenue, the Blue Point Crab House, and Gordon's Crab House. Gordon's had large windows with no curtains down half the block; all the ladies were picking the crab meat and were easily visible walking down Orleans Street. Gordon's had a menu of fresh crabs, steamed crabs, crab meat, crab cakes, soft crab sandwiches, and crab cake subs. How delicious. The local grocery and produce store located at Orleans Street and Milton Avenue would always have soft crabs lying on a table with something like wet hay and pick out the soft crab we wanted. We would clean it ourselves for a more reasonable price; it was a coming-of-age skill.

Steamed Crabs

Courtesy of Baltimore Museum of Industry

COURTESY OF BALTIMORE MUSEUM OF INDUSTRY,
INTERIOR OF GORDON'S SUB SHOP YEAR 1958

*Gordon's Crab House on East Orleans Street and Patterson
Park Avenue, 1958. One block of pure heavenly smells.*

As children, we never went to a restaurant. No steamed crabs growing
up. But it did not take long to get addicted. It was considered non-essential
food at that time. The crab cake sub was more an option when you had
your own money. But later in life, it was our turn for steamed crab. And
once that bag opened, Wow, Old Bay. The tools needed consist of wooden
mallets or just the handle of a butter knife and the willingness to get into
it. The crab house was one whole block of Orleans Street from Patterson
Park Avenue to Montfort Avenue. The steaming plant was behind the front
building; this landmark was closed in the early 1990s. There were beautiful
smells all day during the summer.

Soft Crab sandwich: with mayo, tomato, lettuce, pickle, and chips

One of the iconic smells and famous dishes is the Maryland Crab Soup. Let's keep this soup going.
Old Fashioned Maryland Crab Soup (receipt from Janet Divel nee Vanik)

- 18 Large Steamed crabs with seasoning (Old Bay)
- Three large onions
- 2lbs beef-suet
- One bunch celery
- 1 medium-size cabbage (shredded)
- One qt. Mixed vegetables- fresh or frozen (corn, beans, lima beans, carrots, peas)
- One turnip (sliced)
- Three large cans of squeezed tomatoes
- One lb. salt pork
- One lb. slab of smoked bacon
- 1 ½ lb. beef shin with marrow bone
- ¼ lb. butter
- Four tablespoons of olive oil
- Two tablespoons of Worcestershire sauce
- One teaspoon of saffron (optional)
- ½ cup of cold water
- Two tablespoons of flour can use with 1 cup of barley to replace flour and corn starch
- Two tablespoons of corn starch
- One tablespoon of sugar
- ½ teaspoon Tabasco sauce
- One ¼ teaspoon thyme, I use three tablespoons of Old Bay or more, depending on your taste
- Two garlic cloves (optional)
- One can of crab meat (optional)

Now the work begins:

- I need one huge soup pot
- Pick meat from crabs. Reserve all shells, bits, and most of the remains for the stockpot. Add to the shells 2 gallons of water, 2 large bay leaves, beef suet, slab bacon, shin meat and bone, salt pork, one teaspoon salt, Worcestershire, and one cut the turnip.
- Bring to a boil and reduce to simmer for 3 hours.

- Strain stock, reserving meat and bacon for a side dish.
- Add to a large skillet diced onions, celery, butter, olive oil, thyme (optional), and garlic can use old bay seasoning instead. Saute with half the picked crab meat for 20 minutes or until celery is tender. Add tomatoes and simmer for 15 minutes.Bring stock to boil- add content of skillet, mixed vegetables, remaining salt, Tabasco, shredded cabbage, and the balance of crab meat. Let simmer for 20 minutes. Blend flour and corn starch with cold water (or you can use 1 cup barley). Stir into the soup. I also add an extra can of crab meat, depending on how much meat you get from the steamed crabs. Cook for 15 minutes. Cook slowly to the finish. Allow cooling if you plan to freeze any of the soup.

Maryland Crab Soup

Another prized delicacy was the Coddie, shaped like a small hamburger made of salt cod and abundant potatoes, deep-fried. They were available everywhere, candy stores, delis, bars, and drug stores. They would sit on the counters, unrefrigerated with yellow mustard and saltine crackers. The price for this wonder was 5 cents. Add a Pepsi with that, and we had a meal. No $20.00 lunches those days. With smells comes taste. Start with something sour; another treat large white sour onion, peel the layers away, get a seat on the steps, and enjoy; it was an enquired taste. We had plenty of homemade chicken noodle soup. Also, fried tomato sandwiches or tomato and mayo. Some German dishes whose receipts got handed down thru the generations like kabasa or pork with sauerkraut and sour beef (Sauerbraten). Smell equals culture. A favorite around our house was Sour beef and dumplings, Sundays only. Potato pancakes with mustard or applesauce, and when the neighbor Mrs. Smith would make corn fritters, there was always a knock at the door or a reach over the back fence. She would share with us. She thought my brothers and I were too skinny. Neighborhood caring

I cannot forget the deli. Eastern European immigrants brought the knowledge of corn-beef, bolognas, frankfurters, sausage, and many more tasty foods. That smell was pickle brine for fresh kosher dill, warm rye bread, and corn beef; even with your eyes closed, they would know where they were. Lombard Street was the Jewish Delicatessen row; Attman's was famous. There was always a line outside the door at lunchtime. Nate's on North Avenue from 1935 to 1967, and the deli on Baltimore Street and Patterson Park Avenue gave our neighborhood some of that Jewish delicatessen aroma. Delicatessen's word means delicacies; most deli foods were for special occasions; now, it's everyday food.

French fries sopping in beef gravy are delicious on the top of the food list. I cannot forget the snowballs, an inexpensive summer treat. It consisted of shaved ice and flavoring for those unfamiliar with that name. Spearmint, cherry, and chocolate were a few of the flavors. Add some heaven to the taste buds, with sticky marshmallow topping, for only a penny more. Many of the neighborhood women would create their snowball-type stands. They would set up in the back yard, selling them out of the front, kitchen, or cellar window. No need for advertising word of mouth was all that was necessary. No electric shavers; those days, there would be a large block of ice in your sink and a manual hand shaver. The ice was covered with a heavy cloth to keep it from thawing. The ice delivery service was on Monument and Eden Street. Kitty's mom had a snowball stand using the kitchen window as the storefront, that was her summer business, and in the winter, Mrs. P would make and sell caramel-coated apples on the stick. The idea here was to have a tasty treat for the neighbors but help out with their finances. People got inventive.

Snowball with chocolate syrup and Marshmallow topping. Delicious

The drink was sweet tea, and there was always an old brown stained pot sitting on the stove with tea bags immersed in the water and left to steep. Not much sugar around used mint leaves from my grandfather's tiny garden.

The Northeast Market was our neighborhood bazaar, and it was initially built and constructed in 1885. The building was a traditional style of 1955. The culture of the community-made local foods available every day or Saturday shopping. Located on 2101 East Monument Street, bordered by 601 North Chester and North Duncan streets. Chester street also had stores across from the market and a public bathroom. Baltimore was a place of traditional foods, primarily European style, at that time. Let us go back and see, feel and smell the past and try to get an ikling of how it was to leave your home and not jump in a car. Get their shoes, boots, or flip-flops on and get out that door and, of course, the umbrella in case of rain. Walking was not so bad. We still arrived at our destination and got a tour of what was going on in the neighborhood. Never a boring walk; usually, we would come across a neighbor or a friend. Entering thru the Monument and Chester Street door, we would instantly feel and smell the different environment. The sounds of constant conversations and a huckster's voice yelling filled the air. The concrete floor did not help with the noise level and had that wet look due to washing daily with a hose. The stalls were close together and had hanging lights The wintertime inside the market was cold, damp, and dreary; some hucksters wore coats, hats, and gloves. You could see the steam from their breath. This local Market was nothing fancy. That was never a problem with us; something else erased all that. It was the sights and the smells. Throughout the year, there were piles of fresh oysters still in the shell, soft-shelled crabs on wet straw, horseradish, Dietz Bros poultry with live chickens, and turkeys. Wetzelburgers hot dogs/sausages, german baloney, Braunschweiger, and sold that smelly cheese.

There were several butchers, candy stalls, and Fresh Utz's Potato Chips; you could take the empty can back for a refill. Sauerkraut was presented in large wooden barrels and put in a paper cone to carry home fresh fruits and vegetables. It was a world into itself.

During the Easter season, you could buy live peeps and bunnies. I walked thru the market, coming home from school every day, especially when it rained. It was an excellent place to dry off. There were no eateries at thattime in the market. The market was a vibrant and harsh place where people sold their wares and for people to buy their necessities. All the vendors were probably the 2nd generation; they knew the locals. Mostly the women of the neighborhood went shopping at the markets; they were also the ones who did the cooking. Ethnic foods were still prevalent in the 1940s and 1950s, but as the older generations left us, they became unfamiliar. Our culture was disappearing.

My German Grandfather would put pig's feet in a large jar in the basement, a saturation of hot vinegar brine and Water. This method allowed preservation without the need for refrigeration. Not a pretty sight. Two of the delicious foods, according to my grandmother, were Limburger cheese, which was a German/ Belgium product. After three months of processing, this cheese produces its notorious smell because of the bacterium used to ferment Limburger cheese and many other smears-ripened cheese. I remember my Grandmother and Grandfather disagreeing about why did my grandfather leave Limburger cheese in his coat pocket and hung it up in the cellar doorway for several days. That was a stinky house for quite a while. The German and the Czech community, along with my Grandmother, also ate and enjoyed Headcheese (german word Sulze). This delight is made from the head of a calf or pig and mixed in aspic. The head parts used vary; the brain, eyes, and ears. The tongue, and sometimes the feet and heart, may be included. It would simmer to produce stock when cooled, and the stock congeals because of the natural gelatin found in the skull. Flavored with onion, black pepper, allspice, bay leaf, salt, and vinegar, and eaten at room temperature.

SULZE

The Northeast Market was the supplier of these ethnic foods. The decline of the original immigrants and theirchildren, who used the market as their primary shopping source, disappeared and eventually put the traditional market into that regression. On occasion, there  was music and dancing on the Duncan Street side of the market; the street was closed off. That was the first time I saw the real dirty boogie, Jitterbug, and more Jitterbug was the thing. They had moved with flips, slides, and spins; a dance teacher would have been jealous. We all had a good time. It was all about the dancing, not about who could participate, we were celebrating with the music, and the different neighborhoods partook. How did things get so problematic?

Sunday mornings had aromas that were special for that day. The local bakeries were at full steam baking their ethnic specialties. Most of these bakeries were storefront row houses. There were many bakeries; very few have survived and are still baking. The local bakery that made butter cake was the trendy place, but Hoehn's Bakery, located on 400 South Conkling Street, 21224, Highlandtown, had that cake down to a science. Hoehn's Bakery was opened in 1927 by a German immigrant William Hoehn. An essential stop if you have a sweet tooth and are in northeast Baltimore.

2018

Local peach cake, the base of sweet raised dough, fresh peaches, sliced or halved top with sugar. Baltimore Peach Cake

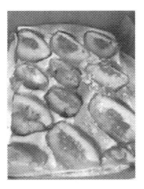

Baltimore iced raisin bread

My favorite, (Butterkuchen) gooey german butter cake, is also made at small bakeries like Marquard bakery and Brown's located on Belnord Avenue near Fayette Street. This one could make teeth hurt in a very delicious way. It's what it sounds like butter, butter, and more butter. It starts with a sweet raised dough, topped with butter and sugar like peach cake. There were puddles of butter lying on top of the crust in the finished product, and the smell was heavenly. To ensure butter cake for Sunday was on the table, butter cake was pre-ordered, and when inside these bakeries, there were shelves full of those white boxes with names. Sunday was a special traditional day; this was not part of the diet during the week. If you were lucky, there were raisin bread with icing, marshmallow donuts, apple and cherry pies, sticky buns, and another favorite honey dip donuts (yeast donut).

STICKY BUNS

Marshmallow donuts were delicious, with lots of marshmallows in between the layers. However, you cannot buy these unless you eat one right away.

When hearing about New York cheesecake, Baltimore has a Smearcase cake specialty. Hoehn's Bakery also had this as one of their specialties; this is a traditional German cheesecake made with cottage cheese. Baltimore's first place to visit should be Herman's Bakery, located at 7560 Holabird Avenue, 21222. They still make a lot of the old classics.

2017

The bakeries were a good sight, and smell sensations still float in my memories. Smearcase sprinkled with cinnamon and powdered sugar and wrapped in a white box with red bakery string. Classic

Apple pies with icing

Some smells were not of the sweet type; people always had the scent of local meat, crab, bread, and various other packing factories. I could see the red Esskay Quality Meats sign on 3800 East Baltimore Street from my upstairs front window until 1993. Depending on how the wind blew, we could smell various meat smells. This place was one of the leading employers in the 40,s 50,s and up to 1990s. Not all those aromas were a great remembrance of your senses. There were others to struggle with, meaning whatever blew our way. Gaseous smells are hard to avoid, like being at the streetcar/ bus stop when it drove away or inside, especially in the back seat; the fumes were tough to take. There were cars and trucks on the main streets like East Orleans Street (Route 40) with no special emulsions control. The asphalt smell was always there; the tar/asphalt. The roofers would be on the payments with a wheeled large oblong covered pot, the flames were visible on the bottom, from that they would put that hot mess into smaller containers and use a pulley system up to the roof, the pots dumped and the roofers used very large mops to spread it across the top. It's a smell you got accustomed to since it was an everyday aroma. Across from St. Andrews Business school was an incinerator with a large smokestack for John Hopkins Hospital. All Disposals burned there. When the weather was warm, the windows were open in the classroom Again the wind was in charge—no need to say more.

The sights and people were just about anything you could imagine. Busy and vibrant are the words. Social Clubs (gangs) started appearing more frequently throughout the city in the '50s. Names like Imperials and Imperialetts, red and white jackets, Joyriders with green and white jackets, Wildcats with black jackets, 7thward, Paradise Club, and others. There were tribulations between the gangs and fights with chains, crowbars, baseball bats, or fist-over turf. The idea behind starting a club was for protection and to socialize. The streets and the neighborhoods were changing into something different.

Muggings were more often, groups of kids jumping others. Usually, the victims got injured. Several friends and I became victims of several muggings, and I especially remember one. I walked out of Gordon's Crab house with my sub, and I felt this rush coming behind me. As I turned, a push on my chest knocked me down to the concrete. I held on to my bag; he was not getting it. I was furious at that black kid, then he ran as a cab pulled on the sidewalk, out of the car came this black taxi driver, he helped me up, asked me if I was ok, there were a few scrapes, but now I felt different than I did a few minutes before. Hatred was starting to erupt; there were stabbings, chasing with threats. A razor blade was now a weapon. They were pushed into the front part of a shoe and had the sharp side out. If you got kicked, it would make a nasty wound. It was not a good sign of what was happening on the streets.

People are now more educated and aware that respect from all sides is needed. We must overcome the past and come together and start anew. It's worth a try. But during those times, it was impossible.

The police could not keep up with the so-called mischief. We were starting to feel a disconnect from the neighborhood. My friends and I had to change, it seemed to get more severe, and we rarely walked home alone. Friends and protectors were the same. There always have to be some troublemakers. Staying home was not an option. Despite the change, the streets were alive, there was the jitterbug, things were happening, and we wanted part of the sights, sounds, and people. Other Transformations were slowly showing their ugly head, and there was more drug activity, and soon it was becoming the norm. Despite some disbelief, the drug culture in the 1950s was heroin, pot, uppers (yellow jackets), downers, spray paint, glue, and other crazy things. The big drug takeover was on its way. People started to lose control of their lives. Those things were more secretive about who did what than they are today. We lost friends and acquaintances. We saw them lying in a coffin at a young age bringing this menace to our doorsteps. There are no heroes in this story. Drugs were destroying culture and neighborhoods. The best thing to do those days was to avoid those involved. We decided to stay being kids and not fall into the trap; not all survived the urge. Now, this is the most destructive force in our country. A recent visit to my city gave me such heartache and made me want to express my feelings:

Succumb
Today I went into my city: today I saw the sadness
The face of misery-for all those who succumb to drugs
A look with a pretend smile, whose eyes show the pain
A body of frailty too tried for the truth
A fascia of total despair, their arms are against the body

But you can feel them extending for help
They will never ask and will probably not survive. Written
by Janet Divel nee Vanik, 2018

Before everyday reality took effect, when we all had young thoughts, and the big thing was to get together and enjoy each other's company, we did. Some hangout places were Andy's and his 5 cents game pinball machines at North Rose Street and East Jefferson Street. Pinball machines, this was a dangerous game to some; at any time, one of the guys would be banging on these inferior innocent machines, cussing away so they would look like the victim.

One of the significant hangouts was the Arundel on North Bradford Street and East Monument Street. Looking for a ride, but not till everybody pitched in for gasoline. Now we could take a spin away from the neighborhood and go cruising. One of the spots was the Ameche's Drive-in at Richie Hwy and 770 Wise Ave. Wheels were available, and we could now leave the immediate neighborhood. We were growing up.

Fifteen cents for a hamburger at Gino Marchett's on Eastern Avenue. They were not only meeting places and maybe grabbing that 15-cent hamburger; usually, the parking lots became the showroom for all the muscle cars. All of this is now gone. Let's not forget submarine watching at Lake Montebello. That would be making out while parked around the lake. Phone extensions were Mulberry MU, Atwater AT, Tuxedo TU, and Peabody PE. They could tell what part of town they were from by their extensions. Patterson Park, located on Patterson Park Avenue and Baltimore Street, was the only country we knew. A Chinese pagoda type was in the park on the Patterson Park Avenue side, which was always a mystery. When I started to write this book, and Patterson Park came up being part of the neighborhood, the research showed a lot of history connected to the park. Why was this history not taught in school? It is one of the oldest parks in Baltimore, with 300 years of history. The first known resident was Quinton Parker in 1669, and in 1792 William Patterson purchased the 200 acres at auction for $8,500.00. The Pagoda sits on Hampstead Hill, a ridge wherein 1814 Baltimoreans gathered to protect the city from a British invasion. As the British marched to Baltimore and looked up Hampstead Hill, they saw Rodger's Bastion and 100 cannons, plus 20,000 troops. They decided to return to their ships and leave Baltimore. In 1827 William

Patterson presented the Mayor of Baltimore with six acres of land on the hill. Later in 1850, the city purchased another 29 acres from Patterson's heirs. On July 13, 1853, 20,000 citizens viewed the introduction of the park as a public space. The city acquired 30 more acres to begin planning a park and structures that resemble Central Park in New York. But the park's idea was to wait. The Park became a military lookout, and on the eve of the Civil War, all parks and open spaces were for occupied troops. After the war, the area needed a complete restoration.

COURTESY OF AAUBREY BODINE

The Patterson Park Pagoda, before restoration 1962

The Pagoda was designed in 1890 by Charles Latrobe. Added to the park's Victorian appeal, one could view downtown Baltimore's many neighborhoods, the Patapsco River, the Key Bridge, and Fort McHenry. The decay of the park was visible when I was growing up. The Pagoda was closed and boarded up in 1951. I remember walking on the outside walkway before they put up a fence. We never went inside and saw this beautiful landmark. There was an option of demolition, but thankfully a project to completely restore the Pagoda was guided by the Friends of Patterson Park and many others. They finished in the spring of 2002. This beautiful and unique Pagoda is alive again.

A playground at the park, which had an old metal water fountain for drinking, had a particular taste but was better than nothing.

In the winter, when it snowed, the kids knew right where to go, sleights and cardboard boxes going down Cannon Ball Hill, and in the summer, we would just roll down those hills. No fear.

COURTESY OF AAUBREY BODINE

In the mid-1940s, there were soapbox derbies; the homemade racers ran on gravity. Old fruit and other types of used boxes were the body. The other parts were wagon wheels, 2x4s or whatever was available, front and rear axles, rope for steering, and the lucky ones had a steering wheel. There was some type of braking system, and it was primitive. Remember sitting on the grass and waiting for these pretend muscle cars to go whizzing by. Year: 1945 Patterson Park

The Boxcars measured 81 inches long, 24 inches high, and 35 inches wide. The year 1926

We were waiting for those soapboxes to go whizzing by. Patterson Park watchers: Madeline Vanik, Richard, Janet, and Bobby Year 1945

Patterson Park
What is this stuff under my feet?
How alien it seemed to be
It's green in color, pointy yet soft
It moves and crunches as I walk

It does not look or feel like my yard
Uncolored concrete and hard
A new experience
An adventure in the city
Four blocks away, not that far
Lies a wonderland
Grass

The park was reasonably safe in the early '50s. Being young, not teenagers yet, we understood that adventuring in the park, that we always went with friends. Looking out for each other was the way it was. Growing up in the city made us street smart at a young age. One of the good things that kept most boys busy at the park was baseball. Thank goodness some people believed that the community with no interest in the children would not survive with any worth.

Baseball was popular; it gave the boys an interest, kept them off the streets, and because they were narrow, hitting a home run in your neighborhood usually meant a broken window. The boys in the area were always told on those tight city streets or yelled at to go to the park to play baseball, Patterson Park. Some of the boys, including Richard Vanik, joined the Exchange Club of Highlandtown Little League in 1954. The primary sport, Baseball, which was right up at Richard's alley, had a sponsor to pay his dues, making it possible for a little boy's dream to come true. In an article dated 1956. The future of the organization itself depends upon certain vital elements.

1. The boys themselves, through their behavior and attitude in church, school, and in their neighborhood.
2. The extent to which adults, the men, and women of the community are willing to give their time and effort to continue and expand the Pony League. Also, most of the boys had a well-regulated activity to occupy their minds and bodies throughout the summer.

The non-profit community service, established in 1929, was a positive experience and guidance for all the young guys. Mostly boys with no father figure in their lives. It was not all about you; it was also about the neighborhood and maintaining that particular way of thinking.

The Exchange Club of Highlandtown and the four sponsors provided enough funds to make sufficient proper equipment available. Fields were made possible by the Dept. of Parks and Recreation and Dewey LeBrun and his assistants. In 1956, the club's paperwork wrote: The managers and coaches spent many hours practicing with the boys. The boys worked hard, tried their best, and were a credit to the community.

Happy times Richard Vanik, 1954, at the rear of 408 North Port Street. He just received his baseball glove from a sponsor. Highlandtown Exchange Club Little League 1955 Champions

The following five images and literature: Courtesy of the Exchange Club of Highlandtown-Canton

The Sponsors who made all this possible in 1956 were:

SPONSORS

Exchange Club of Highlandtown
G & M Scrap Co. - 3700 Bark Street
Lord Baltimore Laundry, Inc - 3710 E. Baltimore Street
Von Paris Moving & Storage Co. - 400 S. Highland Avenue
Von Rinteln & Sons - 2119 Eastern Avenue.

The year 1955-1956 Far-right (top) Richard Vanik He sure loved that glove! Winning the game was an important objective. As the season progressed, more and more displays of good sportsmanship. The Highlandtown Club wrote it. It shows what really should matter and how to create men of worth. I believe that this organization helped my brother Richard and many others become upright and productive men.

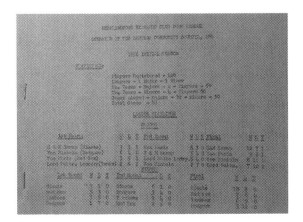

He grew up and learned that nothing was free, first a job to pay for a bike and later a car. This paperboy Richard Vanik saved his money. His first bike was his reward that day in April 1956. I always admired my brother. He always knew who he was and which path to follow to accomplish his dream. Cherished memory

Another outlet for the working class was bowling on a Saturday night. The Spill Way Bowling Alley was on the corner of North Montfort Avenue and East Monument Street. There were huge windows on the side and the front of the building, the bowling alleys were visible from the street, and we could hear the hard balls hitting the deck. The lanes consisted of polished wood. At that time, there were pin-setters: people who would set up the pins, the balls would roll down the lane, and the pins would fall into a pit. The pin-setter (a brave soul) would come out of the pit and reset the pins for the next game. Sometimes a ball would get stuck, or a pin was where it was not supposed to be, and that poor guy had to take his life in his hands. The bowlers in the other lane would still bowl. A loud signal would sound if the bowlers had to stop bowling—no automatic pin setting in the 1950s. Baltimore had two styles of bowling, Duckpin bowling and ten-pin bowling. The Spill-way had ten-pin bowling, which meant a larger bowling ball: the traditional bowling ball had a three-finger hole and taller pins put into a triangular position.

The Dutch, English, and Germans brought their game versions to the new world in the colonial era. It then morphed into our own. Duckpin bowling in the basement of the State Theatre was a variation of ten-pin bowling. The homegrown egotism of Baltimore says that duckpin bowling started in Baltimore. Well, of course. The balls used in duckpin bowling are four ¾ to 5 inches in diameter, which is slightly larger than a softball) weigh 3lbs 6oz to 3lbs 12oz each and lack a finger hole. The pins were triangularly identical to that used in ten-pin bowling and were shorter, smaller, and lighter than their ten-pin equivalents, making it more challenging to attain a strike. Neighborhood bowling leagues, social clubs, just friends or working buddies, families found bowling to be their thing.

Buses and streetcars were the transportation methods for us, but that was soon to change. The boys were now teenagers, time to own four wheels. They had jobs and started to buy cars, nothing new, but they sure loved those cars. Old Fords, Chevrolet, Hudson, Plymouth, Mercury, Buicks, or put-together cars. Some of the vehicles were just primer, looked like a dull black, just rusty, or never repainted. But, what was in style and how much they could afford—a time of resourcefulness and individual imagination. The hot rod was born.

1949 Ford street rod

Sometimes the condition of the cars purchased, and their dream was to have it someday look like this:

Space to work on cars besides using the alleys was scarce. But those small garages on North Luzerne Avenue and East Eager Street, all in a row near the train tracks, did the job. That place was the busiest hangout; they knew where to go if the girls were looking for their boyfriends. Those guys were doing engine repairs, chopping and lowering, doing the work themselves with used parts from other old cars. The real test was to put a pack of lucky strikes cigarettes between the vehicle and the street; it was low enough. How could anyone resist the guy with that limp hair hanging over their forehead, cigarette smoke, dreamy eyes, white t-shirts pulling over in their dream car declaring Hey, do you want a ride? It was a Cruising time.

Above: The small garages as they look today, the Year 2017. The wooden doors are now metal.

Nothing was more important in a young man's mind than working on and having their ride. They indeed were determined to do just that.

COURTESY OF JACQUELYN PULKET NEE HODAK

Proud of his Chevy 1950s style line deluxe, Richard Pulkett
East Jefferson and Rose Street Year 1958 Andy's Store

CARS OF THE TIMES

1950 Oldsmobile Rocket 88 is noted as one of the first muscle cars. Its speed and power created a new world. The firepower Hemi v8 engine in 1951 sent the car guys in a tailspin. "Hot Rod" was the new name for a new era. There is a song, Rocket 88, written explicitly for this vehicle and recorded in 1951. The latest music and the new fast cars were blended and created a culture of the 1950s. Dynamic 1950 customized Mercury "led sled' refers to the use of lead as a body filler in the early days, and "sled" refers to the lowering of the vehicle, giving these vehicles the appearance that they were: slip-sliding" down the highway.

1955 Chevy Bel Air "The iconic car of the times"

PHOTO COURTESY OF SHUTTERSTOC

1959 Chevy Impala

PHOTO COURTESY OF SHUTTERSTOCK

*Space-age Tailfins, along with extensive use of chrome,
became commonplace by the end of the 50's decade*

1958 Ford Edsel This one was defiantly not on the popular car list.

PHOTO COURTESY OF SHUTTERSTOCK

My first experience driving was in a 1938 Plymouth custom equipped with two four-barrel carburetors, with four on the floor, named Hen's Hopper. After accidentally putting it in reverse and going thru a garage door, I never drove it again. Other cars: 1955/1956 blue and white Chevy Nomad wagon with a clutch, 1950's white and red Austin Healy 5 speed with a clutch, stub nose Studebaker with a clutch, a substantial white Oldsmobile, gold Buick Centurion, with 444 engine. We used to call them tanks; they drove great thru the snow. I was thrilled when I got my first automatic transmission car. It's been quite a ride.

PHOTO COURTESY OF DINERHUNTER.COM

Spencer Stewart on an Attribution License

Now, this picture is a fantasy come true, the payphone to call your friends, delicious, greasy hamburgers that were affordable, especially if I was sitting there in that cute little Corvair, my dream car.

The happy days: 1955 Chevy and girls sitting on your Chevy. What more would a guy want from life when eighteen years old? Richard Vanik, back alley 400 North Port Street. Richard worked the night shift at Lord Baltimore Press, located on Edison Hwy. He went to college during the day. My Hero did it independently, with no special funding from anywhere 1st, one in the family to go to college.

The year 1959 red and white 56 Chevy

In the '40s and '50s, some never bothered to get a driver's license. Not controlled like today, Insurance was a maybe or not thing, you break it, you fix it mentality. Getting a license without a car was a tricky thing. I wanted my license, and at sixteen, I was determined to accomplish that and did thru an organization that had driving classes downtown, so off I went by bus to the YWCA. The Young Woman's Catholic Association. I took the bus downtown. There was a blackboard with instructions about driving. Unsure how much was understood, guessing enough to get through this adventure. There was a car, and each one of the students drove out onto the street. Fear got me thru that; downtown traffic was coming, nothing to do but keep going, not looking back. Several weeks later, a neighbor took me down to the driver's license bureau in Glen Burnie and, finally, a driver's license. Felt good. Now a licensed driver at sixteen years old and now an adult without a car.

In the 1950s, suburbanization was encouraged by many local and national transportation laws, which in time ended up damaging the cities economically. The flight out of the city and urban sprawl made automobile sales boom. The car was necessary. Not many buses at that time in the suburbs. The auto industry saw tremendous growth during the 1950s/60s. People were spending more time in their cars and viewed them as an extension of their identity. That usually was the cost, the color, how much chrome, or the condition. That also fueled in the mid-1940's a thing they called drag racing, and in the 1950's it became mainstream. Some of the cars on the road did not even have turn signals. Straight would be a hand up, a left turn was hand straight out, and a right turn arm up hand turned toward the right. Directional signals were not a priority. The sound of the engine was. There were many young guys those days dreaming of the time they would be on the drag strip or local street showing off this wonder of the century. In the city, the guys would go to an industrial park or any straight run of a street, usually on Saturday or Sunday, nobody was around, and they could do the big guy thing, drag racing. There was a place on North Point Blvd that was very popular. Greasers and Drapes drove drag racing, and many others had their own identities. Guys, who loved fast cars, paid for and worked on their vehicles, wanted to belong to something. They looked nothing like the expensive drag cars do today, nothing too elaborate, but if they made that sound and could move with some speed, they were all set to partake. So there was cruising on the streets, sometimes staking a claim, dragging racing a buddy or rival gangs, or just showing off their prized possession. An enthusiastic era, but it sure was full of activity.

Of course, there was a place for the more established racer called Dorsey Speedway, Stock Car Races located south on US 1 on Dorsey Road and Route 176, built-in 1950. This place had stock car races and motorcycles on Friday night. Sold in 1984, its last event on September 28, 1985, with a demolition Derby, seems fitting. Now it's an industrial park. How sad.

On Saturday nights, the old Westport Track closed in 1960.
I did not want to end this part without showing another impressive car.

1956 Mercury

What a beauty, this beauty has the continental wheel, skirts, extended tailpipes, and all that chrome. There is nothing much else to say about that.

During those times, girls never expected to want a particular car, something to their taste. Before the Harbor tunnel, I took the bus to my job at Sinclair Refinery in Curtis Bay. On the way, the bus would pass a Chevrolet car dealership. Something caught my eye one morning.

This little car sat with a beautiful robin egg blue color in the Chevrolet dealership's corner window. This glimpse energized me. Every time passing that window, I thought maybe someday I would have something that magnificent. It was not to be, but every morning going to work and coming home. I made sure I sat on the right side of the bus to get a good look. That car was first built in 1959 and released in 1960 in the Chevrolet Corvair. It was a new concept, a compact car from 1960 to 1969. It was the only American-designed, mass-produced passenger car with a rear-mounted, air-cooled engine. The Corvair's unique design included the "QuadriFlex" independent suspension and "Unipack Power Team" of engine, transmission, and rear axle combined into a single unit. They were similar to European car designs, such as Porsche, Volkswagen, Mercedes-Benz, etc. The name "Corvair" is a blend of Corvette and Bel-Air.

Still beautiful

An essential part of city life was today's 7-11 stores, the small Mom and Pop stores located in the middle of the block or on the corner. Of course, they were always in a row house, but one thing was for sure all the kids in the neighborhood knew where they were.

It would not be an unbelievable story that when the kids in the city wanted something sweet, they did not have to go far to reach this goal. The Mom and Pop stores, all privately owned, were not only a business; they were store owners' homes; usually located at the front of the house. When walking in the door, the first thing we would hear was that little bell on the top of the door that was the alarm system. Next, we would see their kitchen looking straight, usually up to two steps. The house was missing its parlor, old fashion word for living room. Instead of having this useless room, the penny candy store would also sell sodas, sometimes freshly made pasta hanging on a wooden tree, and the other delicious-looking things, but the candy was the main thing. Our Mom and Pop store was on the corner of 400 blocks of North Port Street and 2400 blocks of East Jefferson Street. How lucky for us, it was right up the street. We called the store lady, Mom; how trusting is that. The candy might have something to do with it; she was in charge of that special treat.

Once entering this abode, shelves with small containers of every kind of candy possible on the right side were shelves. The front of this unit is protected with glass or wire so that no little fingers can sample the merchandise. At that time, candy was a satisfaction for the body and soul. That Mary-Jane' would take me to a happy place of taste. The squirrel nut caramels, licorice, a bit of honey, banana split chews, candy buttons, candy cigarettes, Necco wafers, and Nik-L-Nips wax bottles. Tootsie rolls, B-8-Bates taffy pops, Goetz caramel creams, circus peanuts, kits, Turkish taffy, jawbreakers, double bubble gum, etc. Long list but worth reading. We can't forget the gumball machines. I could get a gumball for a penny, and sometimes a charm would fall out. It seemed like there was less fruit and more candy to eat. Special time.

Charmes

Goetze's Caramel Cream candy is a local candy manufacturer at 3900 East Monument Street. Established in 1895, I lost one of my first teeth in Goetze's caramel at the Red Wing Theatre. Best way to lose a tooth.

Neighborhood stores were not a new idea in the city of Baltimore. On December 22, 1907, we had Sophie Kilma's store on the 2200 block of East Eager and 929 North Bradford Street.

Photo courtesy of Maryland Museum of History

My Great-uncle Frank Vanik and his family lived at 2438 East Eager Street during those years. What are the chances that they shopped there? These buildings were scheduled for demolition and are probably gone now. But they have some history in pictures and words in a book that people at one time lived there. Diversity was the neighborhood row house. There were many uses, from candy stores to butcher shops. Of course, the kids had to get creative in acquiring these treasures. They had a plan to make their own money for such unnecessary things as candy. There was no such thing as an allowance. There were ways to make money, soda bottles, that was the right industry to get into; all that was required was walking thru the alleys, looking over fences and garbage cans, and hoping we would spot the big one, a 32 oz used soda bottle, worth 3 to 5 cents, one cent for the smaller one. Old-fashioned recycling was at our local confectionary stores/ Mom and Pop stores.

My friends and I, Mary Ellen and Kitty would have puppet shows. We made puppets out of lunch paper bags or any other materials available and charged the other kids 1 cent to watch. We always found a way. The thought of stealing just because it was tempting would not work. If we succumbed to that tactic, our parents or grandparents would make sure we would have a hard time sitting on our butt for a while. Those days, the correction method was a leather belt, a swift hand, or some other scary thing, the razor strap. It sounds harsh, but that's the way it was. No time out.

One of my nine-year-old jobs was scrubbing the front steps, marble slabs, taking a bath every Saturday, the rest of the week unless something special was a lick and a promise. Running errands, and cleaning the vestibule, the tiny hall entrance. Of course, none of that put change in our pockets. When reaching teen years, it was essential to get a job, when out of school, average age out of school, especially for girls 15/17. Sometimes opportunity would appear that one of the neighbors wanted someone to run an errand and pay for that service. Taking any tip money was frowned upon by the older neighbors. We were looking forward to being old enough to get our working papers, and I did at age 15. Sometimes, neighbors needed someone to walk their children to school in the morning and home afterward. Since I had to go there anyway, why not? I did that for a while and had a runner. She loved tormenting me, hiding in store vestibules on Monument Street, and then the chase would happen. What fun that was, made 50 cents a week. Get a cherry coke at the Arundel.

There was always our jargon, words like wrenching my clothes in the zink, rinse my clothes in the sink—Warsh those steps, and who can forget walking on the payment and wother (water). For the word refrigerator, it was frigadair. Change the oll in the car, yes, spelled it right for our accent. Being from the city, we would say Bal na more instead of Bal ta more. The Baltimore accent is related to the English dialect relating to Scottish English and West Country English. But greetings like hey man were defiantly about the times. Hey hon, hi hon, how are you, saying that word whether to a stranger, family, or friends. It was local jargon there were nick-names like Gypsy, Roach, Fats, Bones, and Meatball that were also lovingly recognized.

In the fall, an indication that the cold weather was on its way, the coalman would be out front sending coal down the coal shut into the little front basement window at Port Street and the coal bin in the basement. This space was about ten feet wide and long, made of wood, and had a gate; it was a playhouse with a door. When the bin was empty, it was a great place to imagine. Yes, I played in a coal bin, my playhouse, except in the winter. During the 1940s and 1950's we had a coal furnace in the basement, my Mom or Grandmother would get up earlier than anyone else. Time to get that old furnace started to heat up; first, there was coal to shovel into the mouth of that giant iron black monster. The following day, you would scoop the ashes from the bottom floor into the ash bucket and put them down at the bottom of the yard for the Ashman pickup.

The main hangout in the house during the frigid days was in the kitchen. Located on the floor were registers, that's what we called them it was a vent; some were ornate.

Below is an example of a beautiful iron wall register below from Baltimore city. Early 1900's Thanks for the gift, Max.

The register had a handle to close or open the vent. The furnace's hot air came out from the grates. The registers on the wall had one in the living room, upstairs in the front bedroom, and one in the bathroom. After playing out in the snow, the kitchen register was the resting place for our wet gloves. Getting that warm air upstairs to the bedrooms always seemed a problem.

We all dressed warm, and itchy wool was the fabric of the day. It was a quick jump from the bathrobe to scratchy wool blankets at bedtime.

Happily, in 1959, we replaced the giant black monster with a gas furnace. Now modern times, we discovered the pilot light at the bottom of the furnace. The problem with the new furnace was that any draft would blow it out, and once there was the smell of gas, or it got cold, you knew. Time to go down and relight the pilot lite with matches, and I will never forget that sound of woomp when it lit. The house was warm for another day.

There have been many changes thru the years in what happened when medical attention was necessary. People did not have an insurance plan. The choice was to go to the neighborhood Doctor; no need for an appointment; the phone was not in every household in the '40s and '50s, so it was a first-come, first-served thing—our doctor's office in a row house on Jefferson Street and Luzerne Avenue. Most people did not go to the doctor unless it was necessary. I recall many stitches done by a Mother's hand. The other option was the emergency room at John Hopkins hospital or Sinai Hospital, located on the 1700 block of Monument Street, almost right across from each other.

I broke my hand while roller skating, and after two weeks, I was finally able to go to the Hopkins Hospital Clinic. It was brightly lit, substantial-high ceiling rooms with rows of folding chairs. Being 11 years old, I felt very uneasy being there, never being in a prominent place with so many people with so many problems. There were cries and moans and the occasional rush to remove people who could not sit in those chairs. I remember the woman in the chair in front of my Mother suddenly standing, screaming, bleeding onto the floor, and passing out. I overheard it was a botched abortion. Girls/women got abortions from any source those days. Because there was no safe and reasonable access to abortion services, lives were at risk. Their experiences are not unique, and even today, women young and old are still vulnerable to situations where unsafe, illegal abortions will become their only option. Some women will die. While I realize that those who care about other actual, living people, with empathy, will fight to help make access to abortion safe and legal for any woman. After seeing so much blood, and the sounds frightened me, I learned to cope with overwhelming incidents. I would put myself in another place emotionally for a while. Maybe I was too sensitive? I was a pro at age ten, having bouts of anxiety attacks since a small child. There was no candy coating for what was happening, and it happened. You dealt with it mostly on your own. I did receive some unexpected help one day, and it was not from a specialist or psychologist. He was the local pharmacist during an anxiety attack one evening. I could not eat, I felt like I would choke, and hard breathing was part of it. My mother took me to the drug store on Jefferson Street. The Pharmacist sat me down and told me what was happening; he said I was creating these symptoms in my mind and how to cope with them, hence breathing and swallowing problems. He gave me a concoction, which I drank. It made me feel calm, and after that talk, I listened very carefully, which helped me for the rest of my life. The fee was zero, the neighborhood price. I am still very grateful to that man. It changed things, I still had the anxiety, but now I knew what was transpiring to me and could somewhat control it. A Neighborhood helping hand.

The John Hopkins Hospital is still there. Sinai Hospital was demolished and moved in 1959 to 2401 West Belvedere Avenue, near the Plimico Race Track. Good health care is essential; it did not exist in those days. The visit to a dentist was only to have a bad tooth pulled. Thanks to our neighborhood Doctor, he knew a payment was not always possible; he took us anyway. Yes, things were much different then. We did not need a computer or phone those days to know what was happening in the neighborhood. Just walking out the door, we knew the latest gossip. The communication device was the people. We knew that we had to be responsible for our behavior. That did not always work correctly for all, all the time, but life is not perfect. There were still incidents happening to us, good and not so good, but I believe all of us would not have wanted to grow up anywhere else.

Where is that starry star?
The one that used to fascinate me on those young nights
As I lay on my bed facing the window
The curtain propelling around with the movement of the breeze
Rereleasing the view of that tiny lighted spot in the sky
I had many thoughts with questions and observations.
What were the questions and
Observations?
I have forgotten them and left them to disappear thru the years
Author Janet Divel nee Vanik

Chapter Four

CHURCHES/SCHOOLS

C hurches were fundamental to the communities; it was a place to gather and worship and was a part of something wholesome. Even on the coldest days, with blowing winds, rain, and snow, the walking parishioners always made their way to Mass. The women were required to wear a hat or scarf to enter the church; requirements for the students at St. Wenceslaus School were to go to mass every morning before classes. They sang out of a Czech songbook till the late forties. Eventually, cast aside was the Czechoslovakian language. As time went by, speaking another language was deemed un-American, and the older people who spoke the language were becoming scarce. Sisters of Notre Dame taught the classes. They belonged to a worldwide religious association of the Roman Catholic sisters founded in Bavaria in 1833 and devoted to education. Their life mission centers on prayer, community life, and ministry.

There was always the question, what was under that habit (headdress)? Did they have hair? They wore black oxford shoes, down to the floor-length black dress, long sleeves with a stiff white collar and bib, which surrounded their head. They wore this uniform during school; there was no air-conditioning or fans . There were many catholic churches and schools for any nationality in the area. The ones in our neighborhood were St. Wenceslaus, St Elizabeth's, and St. Michaels. If Bohemian descent (Czech), they would become Parishioners of St. Wenceslaus, St. Elizabeth's, and St. Michaels and were mostly German and Polish immigrants (parishioners).

The churches were there to accommodate the new immigrants and their religious needs. Many were of Catholic background and were looking for that familiarity. The religious community realized that opportunity to further their beliefs, and they started to construct a place for their creed.

Saint Elizabeth's of Hungry Church is a historic Roman Catholic Church complex located at 2638 East Baltimore Street and Lakewood Avenue. Originally this church was built to serve the German immigrant community in that part of the city.

This complex developed between 1895-1926 and consists of four buildings, a two-story, gable-fronted structure erected in 1895 as the original church, parish hall, and rectory 1912—a large stone Romanesque church building. A three-story convent in 1922 and a large three-story parochial school were an addition to the site in 1926. The complex occupies a city block directly opposite Patterson Park. In 1931, the St. Elizabeth School had the largest student enrollment, 1,500 students in the archdiocese. In the first year, the new parish's congregation consisted of 519 people; 254 were children. Between 1925 to 1951, the most significant growth numbered some 12,000 parishioners and 1,610 pupils. Every summer, there was a carnival on Lakewood Avenue. The street was closed off, with lots of new noises, people, a Ferris wheel, kiddie rides, cute guys, and stands to win that cheap stuffed animal. It was one of those unique things to look forward to in the summer.

First Communion at St. Elizabeth's Lakewood Avenue Year 1960s

St. Michaels Church Corner of Wolfe and Lombard Street 7 South Wolfe Street

Interior Year 1958

St. Michaels Church was another historical Roman Catholic Church complex located in 1900-1920 East Lombard Street. In the 1800s, a Redemptoris pastor for St. James Parish saw the need for a school for the children of German immigrants of the Fells Point area. The two-story, four-room structure costs $14,000.00. On December 29th, the school opened with seventy children on the register, taught by laymen and women. In 1893 a life-size statue of the Sacred Heart was erected at the church. The new stained glass windows, created by Ketteler's of Munich, Germany, are installed. The official language of St. Michaels Church was German. But in 1980, the priest gave a sermon for the children's mass in English. The church added new bells; the largest bell weighs over two tons and is four feet high and five and one-half feet wide at the base. In 1896 the introduction of an electric lighting system, which consisted of nine hundred light bulbs, was installed in the church. It was the largest parish in Baltimore. The bells of St. Michaels would chime and signal the arrival at Fell's Point (Inner Harbor) of another ship full of primarily German immigrants. All the Koerner's, my maternal grandparents, and their children) went to church and school at St. Michaels; there were separate schools for boys and girls. The complex consists of seven main buildings; the Church, Girl's School, Rectory, Boy's school, convent,

Brothers Residence, and the Parish Hall. It was the oldest continuously operating Redemptories Catholic Church in Baltimore.

St. Michael's Boys School Year 1945 6 South Wolfe Street

The Society of Mary, the brothers of Mary, taught the Saint Michael's. Boy's school In the 1800s, the classes were overcrowded. The school was large and challenging to manage, and the boys were unruly, more from habit and lack of education than through malice. Brother Damian Litz, the first director of the school, arrived in 1870. He was also from the same area of Germany, Baden, and Bavaria that most parishioners at one time called home.

St. Michael's Church Girl's School in 1945. In the late 1870s, laypeople first taught at the school, then the Sisters of Notre Dame.

St. Michael's Girl's school Year 1921 fourth from left Madeline Koerner (Vanik)

Imagine a two-mile walk every day to get to school. St. Michael's Church architecture is a late 19th century Romanesque Revival, rectangular-shaped, attached to three to four structures, made of standard bond brick or granite with stone or granite trim. The Redemptorists took charge of German Catholics as part of their mission here in Baltimore. They made considerable contributions to the education and assimilated German Catholic immigrants who produced necessary labor for the railroads and assisted in Baltimore's industrial transition during the second half of the 19th century. No unions then, just hard work.

In 1987 a portion of the original church wall was sold as separate bricks to celebrate 135 years.

1857 unique, touching piece of history

*St. Wenceslaus Catholic Church Year 2017 located at 2111 Ashland
Avenue and Collington Ave., Baltimore, MD 21205*

Now the church building is the only remaining part of the Parish. A
nun's convent, a priest rectory, a school, and a lyceum (building on Madison
Street for activities). The school is now the Maryland Institute College of Art.

There were two entrance doors to the church on Ashland Avenue Year 2017 Use your imagination. To a small child, they seemed otherwordly doorways?

I was a student at St. Wenceslaus from 1945 thru 1953. I remember using both hands opening those gigantic, heavy, rigid doors and walking into the church; there were no windows in the church's entrance, making the rows of flickering red candles illuminate brighter in the dark entry. It gave you that godly atmosphere. There was always the smell of wax and smoke, with brown shiny creaky floors and statues of sorrowful faces. At times, I noticed a serene quietness with a feeling of loneliness and sadness in the church, which still lingers in my mind.

Kindergarten class of 1945 St. Wenceslaus school steps
Janet Vanik sixth from the left, first row

St. Wenceslaus school steps, fourth grade, Janet Vanik
second from left, first row, the Year 1950

The end of being a student of St. Wenceslaus. Graduation from the eighth grade, the Year 1954 Janet Vanik, third from left. It was the end of our childish years, no more schoolyard play; this was now grown uptime. Many of my classmates went a separate way, lucky one's high school. Every morning on the way to the church, I recall the older Czech-speaking ladies' sights having a conversation. They had their traditional style of dress, the ladies who were widows, easily visible, wore black all the time. They wore dark stockings, longer hem-line, black oxfords, and babushkas, and they all carried a purse over their arm. They spoke in low tones as if there was a secret. I did not realize it at the time, but I witnessed the end of an era. Unfortunately, there is no newsreel to recall this picture, but this was part of the sights, sounds, and people that made the city buzz.

Graduation Day at Port Street, June 1955 with brother Richard

The church's namesake was Valcav Wenceslaus, born in c.907 and died on September 28, c. 935, in Stara Boleslav, Bohemia. Thousands of Bohemians (Czechs) immigrated to East Baltimore during the late 19th and early 20th centuries, becoming an essential component of Baltimore's ethnic and cultural heritage. The Czech community In the late 1800s and the early 1900s, Baltimore was home to 12,000 to 15,000 people of Czech birth or ancestry. They founded many cultural institutions to preserve the city's Czech heritage, including a Roman Catholic Church, a heritage association, a festival, a language school, and a cemetery. The population began to decline during the mid-late 20th century. As the community assimilated and aged, many Czech Americans moved to the suburbs of Baltimore. By the 1980s and early 1990s, the former Czech community in East Baltimore no longer existed. That community organized the St. Wenceslaus parish in 1872; St. Wenceslaus is now struggling to maintain its position as neighborhood anchor in radically different East Baltimore. There is hope that with John Hopkins Hospital expanding its medical and research facilities, and maybe St. Wenceslaus, four bells will ring over a thriving Baltimore Neighborhood again

Now let's have a conversation at a more enjoyable time. The Lyceum was one of the places for teens, on Madison Street, across from St. Wenceslaus's schoolyard. Before my time, they used it as a gym back in the day. The C.Y.O. (Catholic Youth Organization) had their events there, and the socials (dances) created a release and did your favorite style of dance. It was a good thing, a place to go, dance, socialize, and be a teenager.

AROUND they go dancing to the lastest records at St. Wenceslaus' Social.

DANCING at a recent social were these happy CYO'ers.

In 1957 the Lyceum Bulletin was published on the second Thursday of each month by CYO members at St. Wenceslaus Parish at 2111 Ashland Avenue. St. Wenceslaus CYO, at that time, had many activities going on. For example, at Roh's, Rockey Point, Conrads Ruth Villa, Shore parties, or activities, past Bengie drive-thru.

They had girls and boys softball leagues and bowling leagues, all associated with the CYO. I was a member for a while, but work got in the way at fifteen. The Priest who was in charge of the dances would walk around the floor, tap you on the shoulder and tell the couple if they were dancing too close.

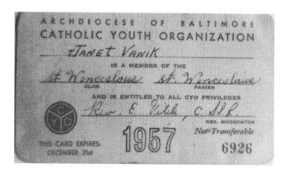

After graduation from the eighth grade, I and several of my old classmates went to St. Andrews Business School, located at 727 North Washington Street, between Monument Street and Madison Street. The clergy purchased the church site in November 1877 and laid the cornerstone on May 22, 1878. The church's dedication took place on Sunday, October 6, 1878. It was a very impressive turnout for a small church in the 1800s; the streets had an estimated 7,000 to 8,000 people. At one time, the school had an attendance of almost 500 children. However, the church building's first floor soon proved too small to accommodate the school. So the church purchased the remaining homes between the school and Madison Street, the large vacant lot at the church and school rear. At one time, there was an Elementary School, Grades 1-8. The School Sister of Notre Dame taught the schools. On the Monument Street side was a good-sized garden, just some tiny trees and bushes, which was an unusual sight in the city; it was the color green in the otherwise gray landscape.

PHOTO COURTESY OF THE CATHOLIC REVIEW

St. Andrew's Roman Catholic Church, 727
North Washington Street Year: 1962

The school was a two-year program; it consisted of typing, shorthand, business English and adding machines, and they believed that the students (girls) were ready for the world. It was essential for us to get our independence as soon as possible. Now at fifteen, the girls were adults. I know now that we lack the knowledge to live to our potential. We thought the future was inevitable. We had no plans, no promises, and no value. It was a continuance of the lack of education and more poverty. Part of the city living was walking to school from Port Street to Washington, and

Madison Street was around two miles each way. No complaints here; there was always something interesting to see.

Graduation Day from St. Andrews for my cousin Beverly Vanik 1959

Beverly and I never knew each other growing up. She did not live in the city. So it was a surprise to find out that she also went to St. Andrews only 2 years after I graduated. Small world. We became best friends later in life. I always wished it was sooner.

Before recorders, a trendy subject was Shorthand. What is Shorthand? Probably something most new bees will not know or ever hear of this. The first time with shorthand, I thought of learning a new language. I would think of Egyptian hieroglyphs and get thru the dull day by daydreaming about learning a different language. I would settle for that and maybe get a better job than anticipated.

The church structures were some of the city's most beautiful architecture, and I would get inspired when walking thru those doors. They brought a visual beauty to the neighborhood. Time moved on, and these buildings were no longer critical to the area, so the city demolished the buildings. As modern times would have it, something square would replace the old. Another neighborhood is disappearing and moving ahead with a lack of visual interest in the future. Of course, that is not always significant to others. Knowing the importance of the future and new endeavors, I will always be a little stuck in the past

Hopkins Parking Lot where once St. Andrews stood

St. Andrew's church, school, and other buildings on this property closed in 1974 and were demolished in the 1980s to make way for John Hopkins's Hospital Parking Lot. Surprise, it looks like a big square building! Well, this ends my school education, and on the last day of school, I remember walking up that hill to Monument Street, the sun was shining on my face, thinking I could do good, maybe get a decent job, get out of poverty, and I took it from there, the best I knew how.

There were traditions, mainly if they involved the church in those times. Every hallway in the old neighborhood homes had this hanging on the wall. It's a holy water dispenser; no buttons to push; just put your fingers in the water and make the cross for a blessing. Elizabeth Koerner, my maternal Grandmother, was part of that generation. She would go to church and buy holy water (water blessed by the Priest.)

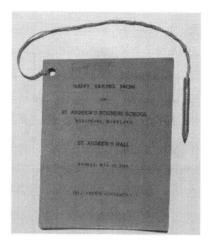

My First and only prom was in the basement of St. Andrew's church. What a beautiful memory. A lovely classmate found out that I did not have a proper dress. She approached me and asked if I would like to borrow a dress. She had two. I was extremely grateful, and now I could go to the dance and thought to myself how wealthy her parents must be. It was a strapless cream-colored flared dress with layers of crinolines, so perfect. I could not believe my eyes flawless and almost my size. I had to safety pin it here and there, but it worked; it stayed up. Many great times and people.

March 1957, the CYO had an event at the Fifth Regiment Armory on 219 29th Division Street, not too far from Howard and Biddle Streets. It was their tenth anniversary. We got to see Teresa Brewer; she was a famous singer in the '50s. One of her songs was "Where the boys are" What an experience there were so many teenagers in one place. I have never seen or heard anything like it. It was music, lots of things to see, and one of the most exciting days as a teenager. Wow, It was my first concert. All the local radio celebrities were there from WEBB, WFBR, WBAL, WBMD, WITH WSID, and many more. Radio was a big deal in those days. March 3, 1957

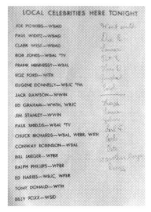

They were famous people's names on the flyer, and I added a few more not-so-famous. My friends were significant, like today. It was all in relating to the times, people, and music. They say music defines history, and it was our time. We were at the beginning of something great, of expression and soul. There was a lot more to come, and that was the Golden Age of Rock and Roll. I graduated in 1956 and got a full-time job. My Mom took me downtown, and I received my working papers at age fifteen, so I would be ready to work after graduation. I was ready.

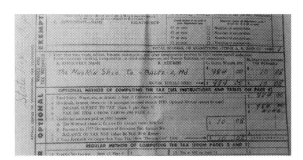

The year 1957 and the 502 Income State Tax Return Tax: Pay $18.90 a week, just a bit of history. For a forty-hour week, that came to about .47 cents an hour. That was my first full-time job at the Muskin Shoe Company. I remember how dark that office was, with no air condition, and that's how it was in all the old buildings. Several substantial wooden desks and huge ledgers had to be taken out from a floor-to-ceiling safe every morning. That was part of my job. I was the only gentile working in the office. Being the clerk and a runner for lunch, I was introduced to tongue sandwiches on rye but could never find that appealing. The Muskin Shoe Company closed shop, and the Oriole Shoe Company appeared in the same building in 1961. In 1979 the Oriole Shoe Company closed. The building still stands, now across is an artist annex at 1400 Block Greenmount Avenue. In the 1940s thru the 1960s, the area was all industrial, lunch pail carriers, and now it consists of several artist communities and apartment complexes.

COURTESY OF THE BALTIMORE MUSEUM OF INDUSTRY. YEAR1958

1950/ 1960's: East Oliver Street and Greenmount Avenue

The Department of Welfare Administration was located on the same corner. The building was vacant after 1982 and razed in 1994. Now there is a new apartment complex.

As of 2018, the original building on the left is still there. Love it.

Chapter Five

SUMMER CAMP –
CHILDREN'S FRESH AIR
SOCIETY (CAMP)

Some dreams come true; the camp was something I never expected to experience. But it happened. Back In 1888, the Christian Endeavor Society of Brown Memorial Presbyterian Church in Baltimore raised monies to give disadvantaged children summer vacations in the countryside; In 1891, the Fresh Air Society was in operation and gave children a two-week summer vacation in the country, away from hot, noisy city streets. The thought behind this organization was the idea that the fresh air provided spiritual cleanliness and was the most proper way to prevent disease. In the first years, the Society obtained vacation homes for children who were otherwise unable to visit the country. In 1895, One hundred thirty-two boys and 348 girls did two-week stays. In the early days, the boys stayed at Camp Endeavor near Bel-Air, Maryland and lodges were available for girls in Mount Washington and Phoenix, Maryland. Then In 1908, the society purchased a 33-acre tract called Dunkale Farm on Whitakers Mill Road from Benjamine W. Amoss for $3,500.00 was the Fresh Air Campsite from 1908 to 1972. There were several rustic frame structures, 15 cabins, a rec hall, a church, two lodges, an infirmary building, and a dwelling. A stone barn and a spring house were also on the property from the mid-19th century; a farm was owned by Jesse Hoskins. Although they remodeled the barn, it is still an imposing structure and was one of only a few stone barns left in

Harford County. The landscape had several small wooden cabins made with natural unfinished materials, unpainted shingles, and clapboards. Interiors revealed exposed framing, no plaster on the walls, and no ceilings. It had low roofs and large porches for ventilation. This new idea of a rustic experience for underprivileged urban families required an original rustic style, and the characteristics now typically provide farm experiences for family groups in the summer. Summer camps were unique at that time. The families or a charitable group would fill out the forms for attendance. The approval of a four-person staff that made the selections and then arranged the date. The Communicable Diseases of the City Health Department sent lists to the office daily of contagious diseases to ensure no exposed children made the trip. Organizations such as Kiwanis Clubs assisted in the early days of the camp. Street carnivals, neighborhood parades, and even snowball stand-raised monies. In 1926 the Fresh Air Society became part of the Community Chest or the Red Feather, a symbol of the United Fund and or a charitable organization in the U.S. There were two articles in the local paper about info for the camp that my Mother saved.

Children listed for Fresh Air Outings; Registration of children who will be guests of the Children's Fresh Air Society this summer will begin today in the society's headquarters at 22 Light Street. The organization, a Red Feather agency of the Community Chest, operated for five periods of two weeks each, the camp accommodating 100 girls and 125 boys between the ages 8 and 12 years, and another article on June 22, 1951. 200 To Leave Today For Fresh Air Camp; more than 200 boys and girls from Baltimore and Baltimore county will leave this morning for a two-week stay at the Children's Fresh Air Society camp at Benson, Md., according to George Y. Klinefelter, president of the aid society. The group will be the first of five to spend two weeks at the camp. They will gather at Public School 99, at Washington Street and North Avenue: where busses will take them to the Red Feather camp. Mr. Klinefelter estimates the society will play host to about 1,200 youths. The notice would come by mail.

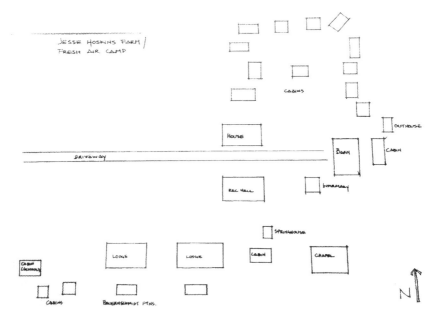

The layout of the Fresh Air Camp

Girls were in the cabins and boys in the lodges

Janet Vanik, age 12, the Year 1953 cabins on the right

For three seasons, 1951, 1952, and 1953 my brother Richard and I got that camp experience; the first year, I was ten, and my brother was eight. The bus ride was scary, boys on one and girls on the other. No one was sure where this place was. After the bus turned off the main road, we headed down a long street (driveway) toward a large building. It was a barn, the first one I've seen; it sure did not look like the large buildings downtown. I felt like I was visiting a different planet. Those days there was no TV, cell phones, or the internet, just postcards for outside contact, so what we saw was what we got. It was learning about things by being there.

After the bus arrived at the camp, the counselors separated the boys and girls into different areas. The boy's housing was on the opposite sides of the grounds. The next phase was a white powdery substance sprayed into my hair. I heard it was for lice or anything contagious. We were de-loused. What was the white powder? Was it DDT? Not having any say, I can only hope it did not harm anyone.

My first wonder was to see a black and white animal in a cage with the name flower written on a piece of wood; she was a skunk. I had never heard of a skunk, and her name was Flower. That was my first seeing an actual wild animal. Discovery There were nine girls per cabin; we all became friends; it helped us forget how homesick we were. We were not allowed to bring the clothing the camp provided. I had significantly loose clothes, including large baggy shorts, nothing unusual, but again we had safety pins. Being on the skinny side, I used them quite repeatedly.

THE YEAR 1953

Ms. Scooter was the counselor for my cabin. The cabins had their names. In 1952 the cabin's name was KAW-LIGA; they all had native Indian names. There was a story going around about a creature called red-eye, it was in the local woods, and  at night it would howl. I remember the smell of all that green stuff; being witness to fresh-cut grass, birds different than city sparrows, strange new country bugs, country roads, lots of trees, sounds of wind moving thru the trees, a different world. I was now introduced to the beautiful wildflowers, Queen Anne's lace, and others.

Yellow buttercups and wild honeysuckle smelled like perfume some older women would wear. With that came the bees. I had never observed them before, or the blue sky, the colors, and the movement. I guess I never paid attention. I never knew ants lived in the county too. I thought they only lived in the cracks of the concrete. I would maybe see a lightning bug in the city on a rare occasion. Nighttime at camp, it was like the air and the lighting bugs were as one. Tiny stars. Many of the sounds of the night became another wonder. Crickets chirping and sound that you would think there was something out in the field beyond our world. Country sounds.

Some days in my free time, I would walk over to the area where my brother was staying. I was worried about him. He was so small for his age, especially in the first year, he was eight and homesick, and I was his older sister. I felt responsible for him. But in the end, he made it through on his own; he was a tough little bugger. Sunday was the day for visitors, but there were never too many. It was a long ride to the city. One afternoon, I checked on Richard on the way over to the boy's area after a rainstorm. I noticed a small patch of ground where the rainwater lay, and something that I recall, yellow butterflies were fluttering around. Just totally amazed. There were dozens all over that dirt. It was one of those magic moments of discovery, new visual excitement in my mind.

What was a day, a week like at camp? A total turnaround of what I knew. Saturday, July 11, 1952, started a storybook about the camp and drew pictures to remember visually to my ability. Not having a camera was not going to stop me from the memories. I was happy. I had paper and crayons. We started the day with rising and shine with a morning bugle call (Reveille), initially to muster a unit for roll call in the military. As time passed, it evolved into announcing the flag was being raised and telling everyone to get out of bed and get dressed. We got the message, and all met outside for reveille. (Flag raising) 1952

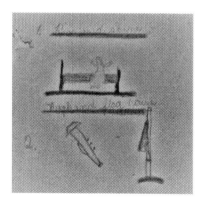

Next, breakfast in the dining hall. There were little cereal boxes, Cheerios, Wheaties, and corn flakes, the box was your cereal bowl, open up the middle of the box and flip the sides, add milk, and breakfast was ready. Back to the cabin to make our beds and do a little house cleaning. The bathroom's name was running waters; it was a building in the center of the circled cabins; that was the next stop. After lunch and the rest period, the schedule changed from day to day.

There were arts and crafts, visiting the humane society, swimming at a pool or bloody river. My question was why someone would name a river bloody. Years later, I heard a very violent battle was fought there during the civil war, quite a few miles from where the camp was. For quite some time after that massacre, people would see blood in the river. There was an introduction to the stage, not Broadway, a small start, more like Barnway. One year we did Aladdin and his magic lantern. I played his mother had a 5-minute part; my words were: Aladdin, what have you found? I was not good at acting; it was a good thing that my role was short. In the evening, we would have a sac supper, meaning eating outside by a bond fire.

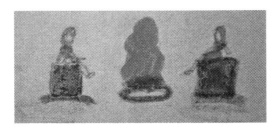

Bond Fire Year 1952

We constructed by hand our carnival with an airplane ride.

We would cook flapjacks on an open fire; I found that strange. Besides the outside thing, they were Pancakes. The best was when everybody painted the totem pole, and I had never done that before. It was quite an experience for all the kids, learning something that would not be taught in school or available at home.

I was learning new things, exploring another environment, meeting new people, and just sharing future memories. It was like a breath of fresh air, what it was supposed to be. At the end of the day, there was "Retreat," a bugle call "Taps," a military signal to the end of the day. Sadly, in 1983 due to lack of funding, counselors' and other individuals' inability to cope with the latest struggles in our city, the camp was closed. Drugs took this wonderful organization down, and who knows how many kids missed the opportunity to see another World besides asphalt streets, smelly buses, and concrete. How lucky I was. It inspired me to recognize there was another place different from what I saw every day. More memories for my mind file cabinet.

Chapter Six

NEIGHBORHOOD ARTISTS AND THE ART CULTURE AT THAT TIME

A Creation of beauty in harmony with a unique soul
Our consciousness, thoughts, and feelings combine to
create our obsessions.

This is Art
Written by
Janet Divel nee Vanik

During the 1940s thru the 1960s, practicality was the essential word. Everyone had to be in that sensibleness of supporting themselves. Doodling and sketching pictures were considered a playtime activities. The Creative, less educated, and spirited people in these neighborhoods did not let this thinking get in their way. They were determined to squeeze out a living from their passion. Down the Five hundred block of Port Street was an Artist who made plaster molds at his house and created forms of people's heads, Fruits, and animals. He painted most of his creations and sold them out of his backyard. My Grandmother purchased one of the heads in the early 1940s and forever positioned it to a place of honor the top of the refrigerator.

Of course, the local guy would do all the pin striping on the hot rods. His name was Winkler lived in the 300 block of Port Street. The Italian lady on the same block created her art in the form of pasta; she always had the fresh strings of pasta hanging in the front window to dry. Getting a little off track, but I'm sure those homemade noodles she considered art. There were the house painters; they were not just painters; they had pride in their craft. They painted the outside wall of the house a solid color first, and then the art artistry would come to play. White lines gave the appearance of bricks. The painters stained the doors and window frames for shine and texture; they used a combing technique. While the varnish/resin was still damp, they would use some comb-looking tool and drag the material around, and the finished look was beautiful, expensive-looking wood decor with lots of grain. That would require a lot of skill, and they were an artist.

One of The most visual arts was the painted screens on the windows and doors. The bright red-roofed cottage scenes surrounded Patterson Park and the local vicinity. Screen painting originated in the streets of little Bohemia in the second decade of this century and was thriving on the streets of East Baltimore is a folk art form and to pay the bills. Back in the early eighties, a count of more than 3,500 painted screens were visible on the windows and doors of the area's row houses.

PHOTO COURTESY OF AAUBREY BODINE

Every older eastside resident knew that some of the best screens were the work of a Bohemian William Oktavec, a grocer and artist of Collington and Ashland Avenues area. Later the owner of the Art Shop. Many picturesque screens have decorated the faces of Baltimore's homes and businesses and well-liked because of the privacy issue, they keep people walking past your window from looking in the house, and the windows could stay open to get that breeze. There were the days when painters would go around and work out of their suitcases. In the 1940s and 1950s, from Boston Street to Monument There was Alonzo Parks, who passed away in the 1960s. His trademark of tan roof bungalows, many in Highlandtown and Canton Streets. Mr. Parks was one of the many street painters who combined his art in return for a day's meal or drinks. He lived on lower Linwood Avenue, never married, and was an actual artist. With canvas, plaster walls, and other traditional surfaces no longer offered. He turned to a non-conventional media like wire screening.

Another name in screen painting was Ben and Ted Richardson, from Poland. They were self-taught artists who painted screens for canton taverns and many other locations. Even in the early 1970's Ben painted a local landmark, the Mid-Way Bar on Baltimore Street. This section is to the memory of a member of our neighborhood. Someone who I would see daily. His name was Johnny Eckhardt. In later years, the last name, for some reason, was shortened to Eck.

PHOTO COURTESY OF ELAINE EFF, THE YEAR 1982

Johnny Eck's "art studio" was at the foot of his stairs in the entry to his lifetime home on Milton Avenue. His easel was the newel post, part of the staircase and the floor held all his supplies. Here he paints a screen for a customer. He frequented the Art Shop around the corner on East Monument Street, where he took classes as a youngster and assisted the originator of painted screens, William Oktavec. Johnny was the screen painter of the neighborhood. He was that half-man, as the kids would say, who sat on the top step of his house at 622 North Milton Avenue. All the kids in the neighborhood knew him, Johnny was an amiable person, and no one thought differently. He was not considered an oddity. He loved his neighborhood and came back to Milton Avenue, after his circus career, to live out his life, a special place to him, familiar and warm memories of the old locale.

PHOTO COURTESY OF ELAINE EFF, THE YEAR 1979

Herewith his dog, Reds, Johnny Eck, at his North Milton Avenue front steps. In the earlier days, he had Major, another small dog that was very well behaved. When the brothers were 12 years old, they signed up to work in a carnival and went on the road with the show; they called him "Johnny Eck the half boy. He was living with and seeing people who had similar adversity, Siamese twins, bearded women, and others called freaks. As the freak shows came to an end. Johnny Eckhardt and his brother came back to Baltimore. They came back to their old neighborhood. Even though the world was changing around him, he was home; how wonderful. My mother was his age, being born in 1912. She would stop and chat with him. She remembered how he would reminisce about his childhood and that old lumber yard across the street where he and his brother used to play. During those years, he recalled that you could sleep outside in the backyard all night.

There was a time when people would sleep out front or in the backyard on hot summer nights. There was no air conditioning or fans. Johnny would talk about his years with the circus midways and the Hollywood movie he appeared in, the 1932 film "Freaks." It was a very emotional and sad movie, but it was real life, at least for the Eckhardt brothers. When John was a kid, there was no radio, no electricity, or music. You would have to entertain yourself. He was using a skateboard before that word became familiar. He took a pair of outside metal skates, attached them to a board, and would use that to get around. We were amazed at his invention. Johnny Eckhardt and his brother Robert were twins born in 1911; they were sons of a dock worker. He had nothing below his rib cage and weighed around two pounds. His congenital disability is called (sacral Agenesis). He was otherwise healthy; it was amazing that he survived without all the latest technology we have today. He walked on his hands and grew to a height of 18 inches. He could not do things other children did physically, but he was encouraged to do art. There was a place where he and his brother would go with their mother and sister to buy paper for paper flowers, which she made to add to their income. That place was Oktavec's Art shop on 2409 E. Monument Street, which opened in 1922. It was around the corner from his house. William Oktavec passed away in 1956, and his youngest son kept the family screen painting going till 1979. Johnny preferred oils and loved the idea of painting screens. In screen painting, the art is directly painted onto the screen and removed from the excess paint from the screen holes. The mesh can still ventilate. The canvas for painting was more expensive, and screens were considered a necessary item during that time and more readily available. We should celebrate the people who kept going, despite what life has given them and did not become a world-famous but remarkable people.

Johnny Eckhardt died at 79 at his beloved East Baltimore home. He passed on January 5th, 1991, and buried at The Greenmount Cemetery. He was the perfect example of a blue-collar family still immersed in surrounding poverty, but He did what he had to do to survive, and art was his survival tool. Now art is an accepted way to make a living.

Sometimes an event happens, and what a pleasant surprise. A few years ago, I carted out an old mirror that, during my childhood, hung over the kitchen sink on Port Street in Baltimore. Yellowed with age and layers of paint, it still had an old beauty. The backing looked like it needed to be changed. After removing the old cardboard, to my surprise, there was sizeable black writing. Almost a complete address, it said Art Shop, 2409 E. Monument Street, Baltimore. The date on the stamp is the 1930s

What are the odds that this old piece of cardboard is still around telling its story about the Art shop? It's the same Art shop in Johnny Eckhardt's memories and the one I remembered as a small child. My Grandfather, George Koerner, also loved art and was a frequent visitor to the shop. It was the only store of its kind in the neighborhood. In the 1930s, recycling an old packing box would be perfect as a back for an old mirror, and that's what my Grandfather did. So being the good steward, I framed the cardboard address. I felt it had an energy about it. I call it soul art, which is an ordinary thing but unique to its owner. Sometimes the past waits for just you, and you find it.

There was another place of art, not local art, but the art had lights on each subject. Patrons could have dinner or lunch surrounded by fine art. Not a fancy estate or museum; it was a restaurant for everyday people to enjoy old-world-style food. Established in 1926 and stood the test of time for 73 years. However, Never were we told what was behind those walls. We were the little ragamuffins checking out the deserts in the front window of Haussner's restaurant, located on 3244 Eastern Avenue. It was a two-story brick building with double red doors and large half-moon windows on each side. From my house, it was a 20-minute walk. I did not know this place was more than a restaurant; it was a real art gallery.

PHOTO COURTESY OF AAUBREY BODINE

Interior the year 1949 hanging on the back wall of this serving area is the original painting of Eugene de Blaas: The Venetian Flower Vendor. A lovely and colorful picture. Shame this photo is black and white.

Looking back, I wished we would have opened that red door and stepped in, and stayed for a while to absorb the atmosphere. I missed a piece of history that was right there. The restaurant officially served its last meal on Wednesday, October 6, 1999. Sometimes we think of places as always being there. Time changes things, and the irreplaceable seems to be replaceable. Demolished in 2016. there will be a six-story high-rise apartment building in its place. I don't know what to think about that, realizing that it is not my property. But another slice of history was taken. History does not have the same fascination for everyone.

William Haussner's wife Frances collected the art on the walls. She bought the first painting in 1939 "Venetian Flower Vendor," by Eugene De Blaas (1843-1932). Over the next 73 years, the Haussners acquired over 100 pieces, one of them being Girl with kittens by Emile Munier, including important works by 19th- century European and American masters. The restaurant was closed in 1999. Sotheby's in New York auctioned the artwork and other estates for 10 million dollars.

Creating art can be anywhere. For instance, an Iron factory located on Eastern Avenue near Broadway was the site of this unique expertise. This piece was created in the late 1800/the early 1900s by Edward Koerner. Edward is in a photo of himself and his brothers on page 42. During the depression, he worked as a garbage man. Born in 1882 and died in 1958. He made this beautiful lady, 5 1/2 by 3 ½ inches, an oddity since she also has a back view. This embellishment was very decadent at that time.

During the '40s and '50s, cameras were still an expensive item to have; there was the film, another expense. But that did not stop anyone from getting an image on paper. For me, sketches instead of photographs were the answer to the moment's snapshot. A little more work, but it had the remembrance. No masterpieces, but a picture.

Looking out the upstairs back window on Port Street 1950s

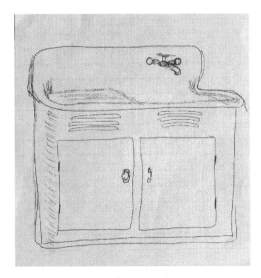

Our kitchen sink.
sketches by Janet Divel nee Vanik 1950s

The artist of Baltimore long ago was not just the ceramic artist and screen painter. Against all the odds, they survived doing what they loved doing. But this is what I remember about my neighborhood; art was unnecessary during those times. After all, the thinking at that time was, how could anybody make a living making art? The bread and butter meant more, and it was entirely up to them how they survived. Our neighbors were quite widely talented.

Chapter Seven

SIGHTS AND PEOPLE THE TEENAGE CLOTHING AND STYLE OF THE '50S/'60S

There was so much going on. Sci-Fi, war, and musical movies replaced cowboy movies, and clothing styles changed overnight. A revolution of change was happening from the 40's style and attitude to more freedom and choice for the up and coming generation. The music change had a significant impact and was creating movement. Even the jewelry had a new look, from charm bracelets to fat wallets. Going steady necklace, with names engraved on the back.

The hairstyles varied with names like the bee-hive, pony-tail, just long and flowing, page boy, bobby-pin curls, big bangs, spit curls, and the pixie cut in the '50s.

The pixie cut was initially called the gamine cut, which is French for "street kid," and it was the ultimate in the late '50s and early 60's. Later on, that hairstyle got popular with Beatniks. At first short hair was not accepted as a feminine thing, but as time went by, it became part of the culture.

Pixie 1962

For that unique look, there were pink and blue hard plastic curlers; what a torturous night. What we did for beauty. During the day, the women wore their curlers and bobby pins covered with a scarf that was a must-have look in the 1950s and usually meant we had someplace special to go that night.

The guys had their thing going on, the slick back, a pompadour, the flop, jelly roll, the flattop, and the real famous in our neck of the streets was the DA, shortened for Ducks-Ass.

The perfect flattop   *The flop 1958*

Richard: first from the right with that faultless DA hairstyle and friend Ray. 2400 block of East Jefferson Street. Who can forget the burly Ford Fairlane! What a blue and white beauty.

The Greaser style involved a greasy hair cream; they had every hair in the perfect position, and it had to be shiny. The guys would never wear hats. In the middle of winter, their hair would freeze, their ears, and of course, do not touch. The comb was never too far away.The stuff to use was Vaseline or Brylcream, created in 1929. John Travolta's Danny Zuko in 1978 movie Grease had that slicked-back pompadour. Brylcream came to the end of its popularity during the '70s, when the Beatles' shaggy hair was the in thing. A little dab will do you.

The Greasers, as some people call them, used more than a dab. The word Greasers is sometimes mistaken for a group of very disruptive people, but the name came from that greasy product the guys used on their hair at that time. The trend was a black leather jacket, white t-shirt, which was a holder for your pack of cigarettes, just roll up the sleeve, blue denim jeans (Levi), cuffed called dungarees, high top sneakers (Keds), and sometimes army type black boots, and we can't forget the wallet chains. Guys had wallets with a chain,which had a leather strap attached to either belt loops or a belt. They were the style and a security thing.

Most of the guys in the neighborhood in the early '50s were either Drapes or Squares. The Drapes were into Rock and Roll, cool with an attitude, cigarettes, cars, and DA hairstyle. Perfect. They would carry combs to fix the do and sometimes switchblades in their back pockets. If they could not afford a leather jacket, the other choice was gabardine or corduroy. Some would tattoo themselves; their hands with the x between the thumb and fingers, or each finger had a letter to spell out words. The Right hand for love, and the left hand for hate. They are lucky that blood poisoning did not set in; after all, they used sewing needles, knifepoint, and a bottle of black ink. They liked to look like that tough, uncaring guy, but that was not always the case. Of course, like everything else, there were exceptions. Another spin-off happening in Baltimore at the same time was the Drapes, strictly Rock and Roll kids. They did not like being called square. They would wear the greaser style. They were the cool guys, the Dad e os. Some wore loafer shoes, chinos with cuffed hem, dungarees, raised collars, pegged pants, zoot suits, which were still around leftover from the 1940s, baggy pants, and Cuban heels

Cool zoot suit 1950's

Chinos and corduroy jacket, school colors, DA hair

Metal taps, once for tap dancing shoes, became a fad. The shoe repair shop would replace the leather soles on the shoes regularly. Shoes were not disposable; they had to last. Now metal taps, called cleats, were riveted to the shoes' soles, the more significant block to the back heel, and sometimes there would be a front toe tap (half-moon). Usually, shoe repairers would attach the noisy new fashion.

Another cool thing to do was to let the metal taps drag along the street or payment while riding your bike, and it would create a spark shower. If the metal taps were not feasible, they would use bottle caps and pieces of metal and let your imagination wander. People usually had a play, dress, and work pair of shoes, and that was all that was necessary. Cleats did not survive as a style; they were too expensive to replace.

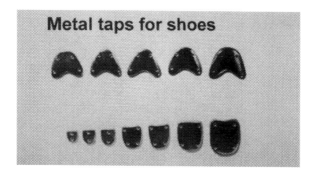

Metal taps for shoes

The girls had their styles depending on what side of the street you stood on; There were the Squares, Drapes and the Greasers at that time. Of course, how large the budget meant how much style we wore. Square girls were the ones who never wore jeans, the guys had crew cuts, and they liked Pat Boone and his music. They wore those saddle shoes, Black and white oxford with a tie, their style. If you were going to catholic school at that time, saddle shoes were part of the uniform, and as soon as school was out, we changed those square shoes into our ballerina slippers or sneakers, Drapes style.

We never had sock hops where girls would take off their shoes and dance in their socks. It was the shoes that made a statement of who we were. Ballerina slipper soles were fragile. They were authentic dance shoes; they were inexpensive then and not made for outside payments. Of course, getting a pair of shoes was not a daily thing, and they had to last. That's when cardboard came in handy, and we would put a cutout piece or two in the slippers. That was the fix for a while. The next thing we needed was the socks.

The anklet sock was not popular; the bobby sock was a white calf sock with a thick cuff, also used as a school sock, so it had multiple purposes. We had to be creative; we would roll down the cuff and put that with a ballerina slipper, a pencil skirt with the cinch belt (made of elastic material, usually 2 inches wide with a metal interlocking buckle). How cool was that? Before the pencil skirts were in, there were the circle skirts (poodle shirts) with the crinolines/petticoats. The crinolines had a flat and smooth tummy yoke but expanded into massive layers at the hip level. Rows and rows of nylon net fabric to prop out your skirts. Crinolines faded in popularity during the late '50s. The new flat style below, Pencil kirt, cigarette, and headscarf, what more did we need.

Della Rosa's on Ashland Avenue Year 1950s

408 North Port Street backyard 1955

Styling with rolled-down cuff socks, ballerina slippers, and of course, the pencil skirt.

Maybe a cool jacket made of corduroy or satin-type material with your monogram in the front and the gang name on the back, a pencil skirt or dungarees, we thought we were absolute. We now need the music, the Jitterbug, twist, cha-cha, slow dance, and dirty dancing.

Special occasions like proms, with that full-skirted gown and the rented tuxedo. This was a big deal and a symbol of maturity.

1961 and 1959

Prom for Mergenthaler Vocational Technical High School on 3500 Hillen Road, next to Lake Montebello Lake Baltimore. Miss Kitty P and Richard Vanik

During that time, tennis shoes (sneakers) became popular. They were canvas and rubber, and it is not like today, paying whatever price to get something fashionable. Styles were limited to a low-top and a high-top, in either black or white. The white was more trendy, and writing on them, names, or other embellishments were popular. That was another way to show our individuality. We cannot forget Peter Pan collars (rounded collars usually with lace endings). You would wear our cardigan sweaters with buttons on the back and that initial pin.

Chapter Eight

SOUNDS, THE MUSIC
OF THE '50S AND '60S

Bee Bop A Lu Lu that's my Baby, Q Bop She Bop, Short Fat Fanny, Tutti-Frutti, Rocking Pneumonia & the Boogie Woogie Flu, Yakety Yak, Rip It Up, All Shook Up, and Whole Lot Of Shakin. How's that sound to you? In the '50s, that was such an enjoyable reverberation and changed our world.

The words Rock and Roll showed its face in the late 1940s with the song Rock and Roll recorded in 1948 by Wild Bill Moore, the sound was called a rocking boogie. By the 1950s, time was setting the path. The Pre-Rock era was over. How did this get started? Bill Haley and the Comets were playing on the radio. Soon new sounds that were primarily black voices were on local channels, and the teenagers loved it. The time was right for music to change to something new and get those juices flowing. Maybe a little help came from Elvis when he appeared in 1956 and gave the original sound a boost because those gyrating hips and his body shakings opened the door for another artist with similar pulsations and primarily opened the opportunity for everybody to hear and see other styles like Soul and Rhythm and Blues. A door opened for Rock and Roll and other artists who would not have the chance to share their gifts. After that, the black artist seemed familiar and vice versa. During that time, there was still rigid racial segregation, and at first, there was an underground movement, and now and then were told we should not listen to that kind of music. Well-knowing teenagers did not listen and were hooked. Now a new way of life and a new slangwitch. Rhythm and Blues were now

Rock and Roll. Artist like Chuck Berry combined blues, swing jazz, and hillbilly and wrote songs about teenagers and the culture that black and white teens found in common. Gene Vincent sang in 1956 Be-Bop-A-Lula was a combo of rock and roll and rockabilly; he is in the Hall of Fame for both categories. In the inner city those days, there were various types of homegrown groups like the Orioles, and on numerous corners, they were singing acapella. In acapella, each particular sound mimicked instruments. For example, the guitar was the Shang-a-la, and the brass sound was dooooo-wop-wop. Doo-Wop was a singing style by local black and white youths; out of the local Italian neighborhood came more sounds. Doo-wop was a form of 1950s rhythm and blues, often compared with rock and roll, emphasized multi-part vocal harmonies and irrelevant backing lyrics. The fifty's leading musical instrument was the blaring saxophone, which brought the music of Rock and Roll together. It was time for the bobby pins to be released, let that hair flow, slick the dude's hair, and go to the dance. For a bit of history in the early '50s, Johnnie Ray recorded Cry in 1951; People thought he was a woman or a black man due to his expressive style. A pattern for later vocal styles showed that racial barriers were crossing both ways.

In 1953 Bill Haley and the Comets recorded" Crazy Man, Crazy," this was the first white rock hit. In 1953, the black group, the Crows, recorded" Gee," a tremendous Doo-Wop song, and were considered the first rock n roll hit by a rock and roll group.

PHOTOS COURTESY OF ALAMY

Bill Haley and the Comets the Crows

Now was the beginning of appreciating new types of music, an awaking baby, that new-fangled music. Everything was coming together, and a larger population was now listening. The cat was out of the bag.

PHOTO COURTESY OF ALAMY

Chuck Berry

This 1950s 45 record player had a case handy to carry from house to house.

For years 78 rpm records were the standard. In 1947 Columbia introduced the 33 and 1/3 rpm record, which held a lot more music than the three-minute time limit of the 78 rpm disc. That same year RCA introduced the 45 rpm record, which featured one song per side, but was revolutionary because it used microgroove technology. Microgroove allowed a lighter tone arm and needle to cut through the vinyl, giving the disc a longer life. It took a while for people to catch on but in the fifties, the 78 became an ancient dinosaur as all the labels concentrated on 45s and LPs.

Now fashion, hairdos, language, attitudes, cars, dance, and kids have come together with a fusion of something that never existed before. Rock and Roll, Rhythm and Blues, Soul, Motown, Soft Rock, doo-wop, we were embracing it all. There was a change in the air. It did not matter if black people or white people created and sang songs. There was a time when that did count. It was during our time, but that status quo was disappearing. Baltimore, like Philadelphia, produced homegrown groups.

One of the most successful and prominent groups in the 1940s and the early 1950s were the Orioles from Baltimore, and they were one of the earliest vocal groups for the doo-wop sound (vocal harmony sound). In 1954 Crying in the Chapel with Sonny Til, he was the lead tenor. Other members of the original group were Alexander Sharp, George Nelson, Johnny Reed, and Tommy Gaither. Their song "It's Too Soon to Know" made it to the national R&B charts in November 1948. The group had a lot of changes thru the years. The last of the original members died in Baltimore in the year 2005. The Buddy Dean Show in Baltimore was a teen dance television show similar to Philadelphia's American Bandstand. Buddy Dean was a DJ from 1957 to 1964, from Little Rock, Arkansas, moved to Baltimore and worked at WITH radio. He was one of the first disc jockeys in the area to regularly feature rock and roll. His dance party television debuted in 1957 and was, for a time, the most popular local show in the United States. It aired for two and a half hours a day, six days a week. Hundreds of thousands of teens learned the latest dances of their day by watching The Buddy Dean Show. Baltimore discovered the Madison, the mashed potato, and Chubby Checker's "The Twist." The TV show was taken down at its height of popularity. The radio station

owned by Westinghouse Broadcasting did not want to integrate the black and white teenagers.

Buddy Deane top-middle

Buddy Deane also played songs that other Disc-jockeys, including Dick Clark, refused to play to a white teenage TV audience because the acts sounded "too black." Songs like "Do You Love Me" by the Contours, or "Hide and Seek" by Bunker Hill. With an ear for music, Buddy also brought to his audience a more comprehensive array of black and white musical acts than were seen in the American Bandstand. Buddy Deane organized and disc-jockeyed dances in public venues across the WJZ-TV broadcast area, across much of Maryland and Southern Delaware. At such events, tens of thousands of teenagers listened to live recording artists and TV personalities. Like many other local TV shows, little footage of the show survived. When Barry Levinson, another Baltimore native, requested footage of the show for his film Diner, the station told him they

had no footage. A take-off of the Buddy Deane show inspired the 1988 John Waters movie Hairspray, a Broadway musical, and the 2016 NBC television musical Hairspray Live. Waters gave Deane a cameo in his 1988 film in which Deane played a TV reporter who tried to interview the governor besieged by integration protesters. Winston "Buddy" Deane born in 1924, died in Pine Bluff, Arkansas, on July 16, 2003. He was 78. In recent history, in 1983, the Essex Community College's 25th Anniversary celebrated the Buddy Deane Record Hop, and Everybody had a great time. We were teenagers again, only for a short time. Tickets enclosed.

In the late '40s and '50s, the big band sound was just about extinct; it was called soft music, slow romantic popular songs, up-tempo ballads, and folksongs. Songs like Gene Autry singing "Rudolph, The Red-Nosed Reindeer, Nat King Cole, with "Mona Lisa," Gordon Jenkins and the Weavers with "Goodnight Irene" was a popular and catchy tune that made people feel good. The neighbors were singing it from in their houses and while hanging up the laundry. Patti Page's "Tennessee Waltz." In 1951 was Perry Como with "If," Mario Lanza with "Be My Love," Les Paul and Mary Ford with "How High the Moon", Rosemary Clooney with Come On-a my House," Tony Bennett's "Because Of You," and Johnnie Ray, and Four Lads with "Cry." 1952 was Patti Page's "The Doggie in the window,"

Jimmy Boyd with "I Saw Mommy Kissing Santa Clause," Tony Bennett with "Rags to Riches," Eddie Fisher with "Oh! My Pa-Pa, Doris Day with "Secret Love." Then something happened in 1954, the Crew Cuts with "Sh-Boom" appeared. In 1955, Bill Haley & His Comets released Rock Around The Clock", April 1956, Elvis Presley with Heartbreak Hotel, "I Want You, I Need You, I Love You," Don't Be Cruel," and "Hound Dog." also, Love Me Tender, another big hit to arrive, was a little known group called The Platters with "My Prayer," you just had to slow dance when you heard them sing. 1957 was another big year for Elvis Presley with songs like "Too Much," All Shook Up," "Let me be Your Teddy Bear," and "Jailhouse Rock." 1957 also produced Buddy Knox with "Party Doll," Debbie Reynolds with "Tammy," Paul Anka with "Diana," The Crickets, "That will Be The Day," Jimmie Rodgers with "Honeycomb," Everly Brothers with "Wake Up Little Suzie," Sam Cooke with "You Send Me," and of course, the square music from Pat Boone's "April Love" and "Love Letters In The Sand." In 1958, there was Danny & the juniors "At the Hop," the Champs with "Tequilla," the Platters with "Twilight Time," David Seville with "Witch Doctor," Everly Brothers with "All I Have to Do Is Dream," and who could forget Sheb Wooley with "The Purple People Eater."

There was the Billboard list, but there was another list, the one that guided us thru the teen years in our neighborhoods of Baltimore. The radio stations, WITH and WEBB, had their list of top tones, Every week, "Top Hits of the week." The hits on WITH had their list of hits for the week of August 1957 was "Diana" by Paul Anka, "A Whole Lot Of Shaking" by Jerry Lee Lewis," Susie Q" by Dale Hawkins, "To the Aisle" by Five Satins, "Flying Saucer #2" by Buchanan & Goodman, "A Fallen Star" by the Hilltoppers, "When I See You," by Fats Domino, "Lotta Lovin" by Gene Vincent," Honeycomb" by Jimmy Rogers, "Cool shake" by Dell Vikings," Short Fat Fanny" by Larry Williams, "Ladder of Love" by the Flamingos. There are so many more "Only Ball Of Fire" by Jerry Lee Lewis, "Earth Angel" by the Penguins," Why Do Fools Fall In Love" by Frankie Lymon and the Teenagers, "Good Golly Miss Molly" by Little Richard, "For Your Precious Love" by Jerry Butler, "Come Go With Me" by Del Vikings, "Let the Good Times Roll "by Shirley & Lee, "Maybellene" by Chuck Berry, "Bo Diddley" by Bo Diddley," What'd I Say" by Ray Charles. Rhythm and Blues, Rock and Roll or Doo-Wop, whatever the name, it gave that satisfying feeling in our musical soul.

Two of my favorites were Cherry Pie by the original artist Marvin and Johnny, put out in 1954 and that Song Over the mountain, across the sea by Johnny and Joe in 1957. I would like to have those times back again, but everybody has to grow up, or do we?

WEBB Am radio station located in Baltimore city– founded in 1955, 1360 AM on your dial. The one to turn on for the newly launched taste and was named after jazz musician William Henry "Chick." Webb, the station had been owned by the soul singer James Brown. It was a black-oriented station, well known in the city's black population with the soul, blues, rock and roll, and Motown. In the fifties, it seemed like the music started to blend; things changed. For the longest time, the WEBB radio station seemed hidden from the mainstream, that time was over, and here they were. With Buddy Young, the DJ, we were generating sounds of the early rockers, Doo Wop, Rock, and Roll, Rhythm and Blues, Mo-town, and soul. Every night thru the crackle sounds of that old radio, we turned in on WEBB for the new old school.

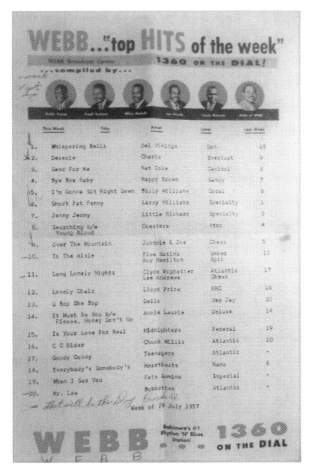

The hits on WEBB station in July 1957 and our favorite
D.J. Buddy Young first on the left side

One of the most popular stores for teenagers was the Petro Record Shop. Teenagers like Terri, who lived on Collington Avenue, would always visit Petro's to see if that particular record was on the shelf yet. 45's were popular; they were not expensive, like the albums.

SHUTTERSTOCK

During special celebrations, the Northeast market side streets, Chester, and Monument had music and dancing in the street, where I first saw the dirty boogie. The dancers were very creative and flexible, black and white jitter buggers. We witnessed the best, flipping the girl over their shoulder, sliding thru the legs and whatever configurations they would think. There were many places for dancing those days, the Madison Club, a two-story house on Madison Street, the Falcons Hall at 610 South Montford Avenue, and Polish Hall on Broadway. Another remembrance of the people and sounds of the city. There were so many tones available, an overflow of musical artistry. Teenagers had a dilemma; we could not buy them all, time for sharing, we would be dancing in someone's basement or kitchen and bring our collection of 45s; between us all, we probably had them all. Jitterbug, slow dancing, moving with the sound of the music. Good times and now we were budding into adulthood.

Time for the 1950s to move over and hand over the torch to the mid-1960s. Many things were changing for our generation. We were changing along with the music; the neighborhoods were breaking up. The kids from the area were growing up, grown-up, getting married, moving on, getting jobs, military draft, going into the Army (Vietnam War), and a recollection of those who got lost in something unexpected in their lifetime.

It was time for our generation to accept the responsibility of supporting ourselves, no more teen dance parties. There was no more excitement in what new song came out that day. Even though at the beginning of the 1960s, some familiar music was still around, it was changing and evolving. The fashion styles were changing; free-flowing dresses, wildflowers in the hair, bell-bottom pants, long hair, usually straight with a part in the middle, afro's, and headbands. In 1969 came the Woodstock Festival. Coming out was the Psychedelic Rock here with the Doors and Jimi Hendrix. The flower children have arrived. In a short period, our Rock and Roll were expanding to a new Rock in town and throughout the country. Out came Blues Rock with Allman Brothers, Lynyrd Skynyrd, and ZZ Top. Surf Rock early 60's with the Beach Boys, The Ventures, and Duane Eddy's "Movin and Grooving." Blues Rock with new groups like Jefferson Airplane and Janis Joplin. Rock American Folk music revival with Woody Gunthrie, Bob Dylan, Pete Seeger, and Joan Baez. Garage Rock, evolving since 1958, with more and more rock enthusiasts rocking in their garages. The Sonics from the mid-1960s were members of this group. New styles had evolved to replace Garage rock; it started being labeled Punk Rock.

Rhythm and blues with Soul was now the Motown label. They started with a #1 hit single in 1961 with "Please Mr. Postman" by the Marvelettes, also included were the Supremes, the Miracles, the Temptations, Four Tops, Martha and the Vandellos, Marvin Gaye, and the Jackson Five debuted in 1969. Soul music developed in popularity throughout the decade, led by Sam Cooke, James Brown, and Otis Redding. This music was the newer version but still relevant to what the 50s teens liked. Funk Rock came later with James Brown, Sly, and the Family Stone. Country music first became popular in the late 1950s, with Johnny Cash being one of the most famous music artists during the 1960s. The genre continued to gain national exposure through network television. Of course, the British and Irish invasion in 1964 helped internationalize the production of Rock and Roll. Other trends, the American counter culture, Woodstock, and current events, became a significant influence on popular music. There were many songs written in protest of the Vietnam War. Written about the Kent State Massacre was the song "Ohio." A few pieces, such as Bob Dylands's "Blowing in the Wind," addressed the Civil Rights movement. Wow, what a transformation, our 1950's generation crafted that advancing ball of rock and rolling.

Hearing that tone
It puts us back in that place
With smiles on our faces
And weight in our souls Author Janet Divel nee Vanik

Chapter Nine

MOVIE THEATRE, DRIVES-IN, AND THE NEIGHBORHOOD LIBRARY

In the late '40s and early '50s, Television was scarce, and movie theatres indoor and drive-thru were famous for entertainment. The outside world, including local and world news, was revealed thru the weekly newsreels in the movie. Now the News broadcast is replaced with advertisements. Mostly in the In the '40s, there was a gray, black, and white film with loud voices (sound), and the whole screen was filled with the picture .A short film of new and current newsreel events, formerly made for showing the news in the movie theatres. The cameras in those days were huge and heavy, with two metal reels on top that would hold the film. The information on such a giant screen made it seem of significant consequence. The news was not that much dissimilar from today. It was not all about somebody's cat up a tree in the old days. The story includes bombs to medical discoveries.

The first atomic bomb test, named the Manhattan Project, was successfully tested in Alamogordo, New Mexico on July 16, 1945. In 1946 the first underwater atomic test was at Bikini Atoll in Micronesia. President Truman authorized the production of the H- bomb, and during World War 11, he had to decide to end the war with Japan by dropping the A-Bomb on Hiroshima and Nagasaki, Japan.

President Harry Truman or 33rd President, announced Germany's surrender on May 8, 1945, proclaiming V-E Day – as Germany submits her unconditional surrender to General Eisenhower's headquarters in Reims, France.

On June 25, 1950, the Korean War began on the Korean peninsula. It started when North Korea invaded South Korea, the United Nations, with the United States as the principal force along with the Soviet Union assistance and China coming to the aid of North Korea, the war ended on July 27, 1953, with thousands of American soldiers wounded or killed. The end resulted in a cease-fire armistice. I hate to say this but does this sound familiar. It just never ends.

Good news March 26, 1953, American medical researcher Dr. Jonas Salk announced on a national radio show that he had successfully tested a vaccine against poliomyelitis. This virus causes the crippling disease of polio. The scary thing about this was in In 1954, clinical trials using the Salk vaccine And a placebo began on nearly two million American schoolchildren. In 1955, once the vaccine was effective and safe, the nationwide inoculation campaign began. I remember seeing a young boy in an iron lung placed by the front window of his home. He would look back with his big eyes in the mirror above his head. I can still remember the sound; it was endless; the noise sounded like a machine breathing, and that is what it was. One day on my usual route, I passed by the house. He was no longer there; the window was empty. I knew what that meant. The memories of knowing someone who contracted polio were a sad ordeal and left many children crippled for life. Thanks to researchers, a cure happened.

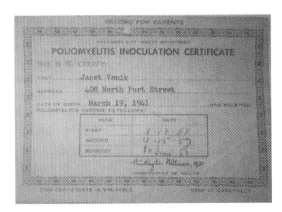

Certification of my polio vaccination

This is a small sample of some of the day's big news.

THE NEIGHBORHOOD MOVIE THEATRES

The Roxy Theatre, located at 2239 East Fayette Street, was my earliest memory of a local movie theatre. This location first opened up in early 1917. It was then called the Fayette theatre, equipped with the Kimball's organ changed into a bowling alley in 1931. It reopened in October 1932 – closed in 1957, and like most of the old movie theatres that are no longer in use, converted to a church. The demise of this theatre was due to several problems. During those years, scalp ringworms and head lice seemed rampant, and the story in the neighborhood was that the Roxy had an infestation of critters, one of them being scalp ringworms, because of the old seats. In the '40s and '50s, the treatment was to get your head shaved and wear a stocking cap; usually, the cap was the bottom of a pair of stockings and tied to create a cap. There were boys in my class with those stocking caps on. It is now treatable with an antifungal cream.

Before computers and television, people had a selection of movie theatres within walking distance. There was The Avenue 1921-1958, The Aurora 1910-1978, The Biddle 1943-1973, Earle Theatre 1937-1970, Hilton 1941-1951, Highland 1940-1951, the Linwood 1916-1952. The closest movie theatre for us during the early and mid-'50s was the Red Wing, 901 capacity with itchy seats. The older places had seats covered with horsehair or a wool-type fabric. The theatre opened in 1914, located at 2239 East Monument Street and Patterson Park Avenue. My Mom would bring my brothers and me to the theatre. We were regulars on Saturday afternoon. Cowboy movies were the big thing at that time. There was an usher. His job was to walk down the aisle with a flashlight and escort people to their seats. Also, check out any problems with noise or anyone misbehaving, for example sneaking in the back door. Now and then, he would ask to see someone's ticket. He wore a small, dark blue railroad hat, gloves, and a dark short jacket and pants. Indeed it was not a pleasant job. There was always some wise guy making fun of him; he was from the past; the new kids on the block did not understand the old culture. In the 1950s, the ushering job was obsolete. Driving past the Red Wing, I could not help but remember the movies and how many times we, as kids, walked to Monument street.

PHOTO COURTESY OF FRANK DURKEE

The Red Wing Theatre: 1940'/ 1950s Monument and Patterson Park Avenue

This site where the Red Wing theatre was is now a store of some sort and is non-recognizable. But I did notice on my last visit to the city that the beautiful red brick wall on the Patterson Park side looks untouched. I can only hope that someone will appreciate a culture there at one time. Recalling sitting in this last place brings to mind those sounds, smells, sights, and people have gone but are still noteworthy. Here she is, that red brick wall I snapped this photo of in 2018.

Cowboy and Indian pictures shown at the Red Wing theatre. Roy Rodgers and Dale Evans with horse Trigger as shown, Gene Autry, Hopalong Cassidy, Smiley Brunette. Suddenly these movies had competition. There was now Sci-Fi, my favorite; finally, something I enjoyed watching, looking ludicrous and comical at times compared to today. All those low-budget space movies had fake-looking aliens, men in suits and hats, ladies wore dresses and heels, and everyone smoked cigarettes. It was all part of the culture at that time. It sure had its Wow factor, "Flying Saucers," people were looking up at the night sky from the bedroom windows after seeing the unimaginable. A new happening in the early '50s, called science fiction with fantasy and something to stimulate your mind. I always thought of it as a future-telling machine. It seemed possible. Destination Moon (1950) this movie came out 19 years before the actual landing on the moon, and it was about a maiden voyage to the moon. How about that, POSSIBLE, remember July 20th, 1969, Apollo 11

The Day the Earth Stood Still (1951) A message was sent to earth for the earthlings about their doom. There was Gort, the giant robot; he was the protection for the alien named Rennie. There was a classic extraterrestrial movie line, "Klaatu Barada Nikto," Rennie said quite frequently.

A remake of this movie came out in 2008 and became a blockbuster at the box office. The Invaders from Mars from 1953 also had a remake in 1986 with the part of the small boy in the original version now playing the police chief. 1953 It Came From Outer Space, a spaceship crashes in the Arizona desert. Local townspeople start acting strange. An amateur astronomer and a teacher suspect it's the alien's deeds.

PHOTO COURTESY OF ALAMY

The War of the Worlds movie came out in 1953. But this alien invasion novel was written in 1938 by H.G. Wells. Once I saw the film, it changed everything. I defiantly became a big special effects fan. Now special effects are more convincing, but it was all we had in those days. With Director Steven Spielberg, Tom Cruise did a retelling of this Sci-Fi classic in 2005. I loved the new version also; it had improved special effects. This movie had one of the bombshell endings to any other Sci-Fi story. A Cold! In 1954, we had Them, giant mutated Ants, one of the first big bug movies, black and white. Their size enlarged by radiation, an entertaining movie with a new perspective on what the future man could bring. Remember, it's 1954.

Forbidden Planet in 1956 was the first film to portray a starship going faster than sound speed. The starship crew investigates a deserted planet, Altair IV, and finds a scientist/ doctor and his beautiful young daughter with their robot. Named Robbie, with its rotating ears, he could speak 188 languages. He had a personality; imagine that. Of course, who could forget the Invasion of the Body Snatchers in 1956, aliens duplicate humans and take over the population of a small town. The alien had no emotions. That's how the townspeople knew who the non-aliens were. The props were large egg cases, human size. The Incredible Shrinking Man (1957), a businessman exposed to radiation and insecticide, starts shrinking and cannot stop. Imagination was hitting all genres those days. This film inspired 1981 The Blob stared at the young Steve McQueen, in his feature film debut, and the heartthrob of mine and all the teenage girls. The action starts with the usual meteorite crashing to the earth. Inside this space, rock was a red destructive, acidic blob. A curious farmer takes a stick and opens the meteorite, and the Blob attaches itself to his hand, which consumes and dissolves the body of the humans in the small community of Phoenixville. With a large appetite, it eventually becomes more all-encompassing. However, thanks to the local teenagers who saved the day, they electrocuted the Blob.

That year also brought us The Fly, plus the return of the fly, a scientist who mutates into a grotesque human fly. It was a human head with a fly body. He experimented with a transportation machine in which a fly flew into the machine with him, resulting in their atoms mixing. At the end of the movie, this creature fly's in a spider web, and with a pitiful sound, he screams," Help Me." Since everyone was just introduced to science fiction, their minds were like babies and had to toughen up for screams and a different way of seeing movies. We did with pleasure.

Musicals were also starting to appear; they had music, dancing, and excellent color (Technicolor), a new thing. After seeing (Singing in the Rain) in 1952 with Gene Kelly, Debbie Reynolds, and Donald O'Conner, I found another love. I was eleven years old and sang that song all the way home from the movie theater. Weeks later, still singing and dancing around the house.

The big competition to the Red Wing Theatre was The State Theatre opened on April 16, 1927. It was located on 2045 East Monument Street, just several blocks away, between Castle and Chester Street. When it opened, equipped with a Wurlitzer two theatre organ. It had one screen, a large stage, an orchestra pit, extravagant decorations, a stage curtain, a vast second-floor balcony, an enormous chandelier, seated 1,860 patrons, and in the basement, there was a 20-lane bowling alley. In the late In the 1940s, the State featured vaudeville shows; dog acts, monkey acts, dancers, and jugglers. The orchestra pit was several musicians playing the music. Vaudeville ended in the 1950s. I feel lucky to have seen this unique form of entertainment. When living in the city, there were many more opportunities for this to happen. The children had independence and self-discovery, everyone walked to places, and we grew up fast, and in doing that, we were much more acquainted with our surroundings and safety. I feel that it was a fantastic adventure.

PHOTO COURTESY OF FRANK DURKEE

State Theatre late 1940's

Interior

This balcony was a teen couple's favorite spot; there was always a couple tucked up at the back wall. There was an orchestra pit in front of the screen in the 1950s; we did not realize this was the past grandeur, and we saw it in our young lives. This beautiful old building closed on December 1, 1963, and became the New Refuge Deliverance Holiness Church. Since then, the building has become an office building belonging to John Hopkins Hospital. Glad they did not demolish the exterior. There was a camera shop next to the State theatre; they sold View-Masters and the round paper Inserts. My mother would take us there, and it was one of those big deals. We loved going there and investigating what was new. Buying an insert was rare, but when we did, that walk home was extra long. We could hardly wait to get home and view the latest pictures.

There was no shortage of theatres in the area, including the Grand on 508 South Conkling Street, Highlandtown.

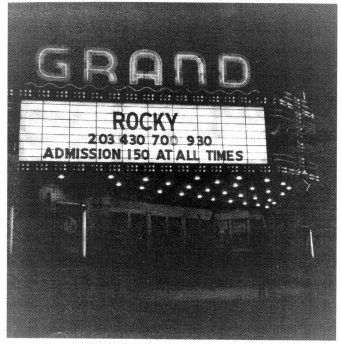

PHOTO COURTESY OF FRANK DURKEE

Nighttime marquee

PHOTO COURTESY OF FRANK DURKEE

*This theatre opened in 1911, closed in 1985, and
was demolished in December 2003.*

PHOTO COURTESY OF FRANK DURKEE YEAR 1940S

*Opening on May 14, 1921, with 790 seats, on one floor and designed
by architect William Sparkin was the Belnord Theatre.*

It was located on 2706 Fayette Street, right where Pulaski Hwy and
Fayette Street join together. Originally the Belnord had a three-manual
Kimball organ. Later in October 1921, a 400-seat. The theatre closed
in the fall of 1969 and was converted to a supermarket, then a mattress/
furniture store. The balcony and upper parts of the auditorium were still
intact, behind a false ceiling. The past is like a piece of our soul put on
the back burner. Then one day, it will become significant enough to be
revealed.

Another relevant theatre was the Patterson Theatre, located on 3136
Eastern Avenue, which opened in 1910, was renovated and reopened in
1920 as the new Patterson. This building was a beacon in the night.

PHOTO COURTESY OF FRANK DURKEE

The year 1940, The Patterson Theatre

The Theatre in the early days had a second-floor dancehall with a stage and organ. That version of this theatre closed in 1929. Later in 1930, it was just a plain red brick exterior but boasted a very ornate vertical sign. The patrons would have difficulty getting lost with the sign's lighting. We knew actually where Patterson Park avenue was even blocks away by seeing that light. The interior was just as pleasing for the times as those front lights. The color scheme included gold, red, and orange with matching draperies. Crystal chandeliers hung from the ceiling. In the mid-fifties, décor changed. The theatre was able to set up to 1,500 customers. A problematic setback came to this building in 1958 when a fire created extensive damage. In 1975 the space was split into two 500 seating spaces. In 1995 this building received another chance at life.

PHOTOS COURTESY OF CREATIVE ALLIANCE JOSH KOHN

The year 2021

Creative Alliance, which is a community organization, saved this building. After millions of dollars, the renovations were complete; it is now a multi-purpose center with a dining room, artist studios, a lounge, galleries, and a flexible theatre. They could not save the old vertical sign; it was duplicated and replaced. I Love that idea. It reopened in 2003. Congratulations on that idea. The love of art and history saved this icon.

During the 1950s, when we were teenagers, the Drive-In Theatres were a new happening. Our generation of young car owners came of age, indoor versus outdoor movies; our entertainment priority changed quickly. After getting a driver's license and a set of wheels, the drive-in teen experience was eager to start. The next step was pitching in for admission and gas.

They were not the days of big green stuff in your pocket. You could fill up a car with friends for less than three dollars. Donation was usually 25 cents apiece.

PHOTO COURTESY OF SHUTTERSTOCK

A Drive-in theatre consisted of a large outdoor movie screen and a concession stand, which included hot dogs, popcorn, and soda; there were no nachos with cheese in those days. There was a playground in front of the screen, making it easy to watch the little ones while watching the movie, picnic tables, a Projection booth and a large parking area for automobiles. Within the enclosed space, customers can view movies from the privacy and comfort of their cars. Originally the movie sound was provided by speakers on the screen and later by an individual speaker hung from the window of each vehicle. It was attached by a wire. In 1941, RCA introduced in-car speakers with separate volume controls, which solved the noise pollution issue and provided good sound to drive-in patrons.

There is some history of the drive-in theatres; strangely enough, there was a type of drive-in theatre opened in New Mexico in April 1915, partly a seated auditorium and also a place for automobile patrons to see the picture on the theatre grounds that did not work out too good closed in 1916. In 1921 in Comanche, Texas, they issued permits to project movies downtown on the sidewalls of the buildings. They were silent films, so the sound was not an issue. In 1920, "outdoor movies." became popular summer entertainment.

Back in 1932, a young entrepreneur named Richard Hollingshead, a movie buff, thought of the idea of a theatre in a park later called drive-in.

People could sit in the comfort of their cars in the open air. Hollingshead family owned and operated the R.M. Hollingshead Corporation Chemical plant in Camden He experimented in the driveway of his home with different projectors and sound procedures. He mounted a 1928 Kodak projector on the hood of his car, attaching a screen to some trees and putting a radio behind the screen for sound. Richard Hollingshead received a patent in May 1933 and opened Park In theatres, Inc., located on Admiral Wilson Boulevard in Pennsauken Township, Camden, New Jersey. His investment of $30,000 opened the park. The charge was 25 cents per car and 25 cents per person, with no group paying more than one dollar. It offered 400 slots and a 40 by 50 ft. Screen. Early drive-in theatres had to deal with sound issues. The original Hollingshead drive-in had speakers installed on the tower itself, which caused a sound delay affecting moviegoers at the rear of the drive-in's field. The glory days were in the late 1950s to mid-1960. There were 4,000 theatres across the country. They were American cultural icons. Today, fewer than 500 drive-in theaters survive in the United States, at last count. The Drive-in theatres were new to the teenagers; it was nonconformity of the past, their friends or boyfriend separated from the rest of the moviegoers, just by a car door, but still a feeling of just them being themselves.

The Edmondson opened in 1954, located on 6000 Baltimore National Pike in laypeople's terms. It was on Route 40, Pulaski Highway, in our neighborhood Orleans Street. It closed in 1991. Now it is a Home-Depot. But in the fifties and mid-sixties, there was a large red split arrow on the

Edmondson sign luring you to the drive-in. It had all the usual large screen, playground, concession stand, and parking for 1,200 cars.

The essential part was the speakers that stood on poles and would hang on the car's driver's side. One of the big problems was patrons breaking the driver's window because they forgot about the speakers were hanging there when they were leaving.

Pulaski Drive-in theatre, located in the 11300 blocks of Pulaski Highway, had the necessities that a Drive-in required. Except for the designs of the sign, the theatre looked a lot like the Edmondson Drive-In, and was named after a famous person. After curiosity got the best of me, I checked into this guy. His name was Casimir Pulaski, and he was born in Warsaw, Poland, on March 6, 1747; he was a polish Nobleman. He became one of the leading military commanders in Europe against the Russians in the War of the Bar Confederation. Casimir became exiled after the failure of the uprising. After being endorsed by Benjamin Franklin, he emigrated to North America to help with the Revolutionary War. He was a Freemason/ Master Mason. He was known to have saved George Washington's life during the war. He became a U. S. Brigadier General in the Continental Army, created the Pulaski Cavalry Legion, and reformed the Calvary. At the battle of Savannah, Ga., against the British forces, he was wounded and died shortly after, on October 11, 1779; he was 34 years old. This statue of Casimir Pulaski is located in the southeast corner of Patterson Park, completed in 1951, thanks to the Polish community at that time.

South Linwood and Eastern Avenue

After many years of discussion and other reverence, Congress passed a joint resolution conferring honorary U. S. citizenship on Pulaski in 2009, sending it to President Barack Obama for approval. He duly signed it on November 6, 2009, making Pulaski the seventh person so honored. He never married and had no descendants, and was buried in Monterey Square, Georgia. A DNA test revealed that the person buried in Georgia was General Pulaski and reinterred with military honors in 2005. Restored in 2002. It was of great satisfaction finally knowing who he was after walking past this statue many times as a child and hearing his name throughout my childhood, such as Pulaski Highway. The Pulaski Drive-in Theatre demolished in1985, now is a run-off pond for water with one steel support remaining on Rt. 40. So much history around us but forgotten.

Another one bites the dust.

The Bengies Drive-in on 3417 Eastern Blvd. 21220. It opened in June

1956 and surprisingly still exists. The historic site does not have a sizeable blinking arrow, and the front of the sign is different from than in 1956, but even had its 35mm projector, till converted to digital in 2013.

The last theatre in the area was the North Point Drive-in, was located at 4001 North Point Blvd and Battle Grove Roads, Dundalk, 2122. Opened in June 1948, it had one giant screen and the capacity for 650 cars. The drive-in was torn down in 1982 and became a flea market, and for quite a few years, it was an empty field till recently, there was new construction on the site.

Teenagers of the day made their rounds of the local drive-ins in their old fords, chevies (Chevrolet), or old Oldsmobubble (Oldsmobile). That Olds was the best, and everybody could fit in that huge backseat. Just another perfect memory.

The Old Enoch Pratt Free Library Branch 13,
the front was facing Linwood Avenue

There was a place with no movies, but an exciting and fantastic space with lots of beautiful books, with pictures. It had that old smell of dusty paper mixed with time. The building was from the early 1900s. Located at Linwood and Fayette Street. The library was down the street from the Belnord theatre. The Enoch Pratt Free Library is a free public library system in Baltimore. The central branch and first to be built around 1886, located at 400 Cathedral Street. The realization began in January 1882 by Enoch Pratt (1808-1896), a philanthropist, banking, and steamship executive, who presented gifts of a central and four branch library to the city. Mr. Pratt was a very frugal man, and the story is that several 1820-era row houses were to be demolished for his new city library. He insisted on recycling the bricks from the homes destroyed. They were knocked off, cleaned, and used for building a hall and parish house for his church, the Independent Church of Baltimore, now the First Unitarian Church of Baltimore. Due to the continually expanding collection, the library outgrew its space and restored the historic Central Library from January 1933. Still again, growing in 2016, another new restoration. He had a vision of a free library, so all people, rich or poor to take a book, read, and return it to the library. In my opinion, he was one of our first educators in the city school system. Libraries are different today; they offer much more than just books. But those days, that was all we had, and happy with that. First, you would encounter two large doors. What was with all these giant doors? It seemed that in every place I liked to visit, you had to use some muscle to get in. It was not very bright, and most lights came from the windows. All these old buildings had an odor of dust. There was a wall filled with tiny brown drawers; it was top-secret what was in them. The librarian would never let any children open those small drawers with the information cards. As a child, I spent quite a bit of time wandering through those tiny passageways thru the tall bookcases. I found this one of my favorite places to stir the imagination. We never had TVs, computers, or books.

So the place to go was the library, where we would get a book to take home for a brief time. One particular book that I did read was Kon-Tiki, a story of an explorer, Thor Heyerdahl, who thought that Indigenous South Americans populated Polynesia, and he was out to prove it. He and five other men built a large balsawood raft, similar to an original craft used in the south pacific. They set sail in 1947 from Peru and made it to their destination, proving his theory was correct. Most of this book I did not understand at the time, but it seemed to be an exciting adventure. I was not a great reader but mostly wanted to see the pictures of the planets, dinosaurs, ancient worlds, Egypt, the pyramids, and rocks. The images were astonishing to me. I think that I had an interest in many things, so I could never concentrate on one.

Sometimes I would think how great it would be to find a tomb full of treasures, to find a beautiful colorful rock, not a city rock, or to travel to the stars. I always had these thoughts. My mind was always busy, and maybe that got me through school, which never had any interesting subjects, like Religion, which included a color book, and we had to color the pictures. I knew that I was being taught and educated enough to get a clerical job, become a Nun, or a catholic wife. The library opened my mind to something different, more exciting, and a great place to imagine other sites and maybe a different life. At the same time, we knew how far we would go; being a girl and unable to afford higher education, I could dream with my imagination. I was not completely broken. There were severe difficulties, but writing this book is one of my considerations to tell the history of how it was for us. Things are much

different today; through education, girls have choices. In 1990, the old library was closed for extreme renovations. In January 1994, the newly renovated library opened, and the front entrance is now where the back door was. This picture shows the new front façade. This way, it has a green space for the front door, not a narrow pavement on a busy street. What a boast for the neighborhood. The year 2018

Chapter Ten

SHOPPING LOCAL
AND DOWNTOWN

I n the 1940s, 1950s, and early 1960s, try to imagine no large shopping malls, no ten different named stores with the same items, no specialty sneaker stores, no credit cards, no parking the car nearby, no going on the computer or phones. During that time, it was a world of buses and streetcars and good old fashion walking, and we did not forget the umbrella. In the 1960s, a change was on its way, and more. Local shopping was still possible.

On special occasions, there was downtown. Cars were on their way to becoming very popular, and people were on their way to more job opportunities in the city's outskirts. Factories were closing in the city, and the suburban areas were defiantly building up, and the change was here. New neighborhoods were moving outside the city, but nothing like the old ones. Joppa town, a bedroom community near Baltimore, was established in 1961 as a planned unit development located in southwestern Harford County. Now customers would have the convenience of driving their vehicle to new shopping centers opening up in the area where the new bedroom communities were. No more waiting on the street corners for the bus or streetcar. People were changing their habits of shopping. Downtown, as a shopping destination, was dying slowly.

There was no impulse buying those days; it was shopping for a particular item, a coat, shoes, or something necessary. Shoppers were more frugal then. A budget was a budget, and purchases were cash or lay-a-way. There was no such thing as pay tomorrow, except maybe in the local grocery store if you had an account. It was a particular time, a style, a culture, and a way of life gone. It is now just a recollection in our minds. During those years, there was anticipation for visiting downtown, that special place with people chatting, traffic, large buildings, lights, beautiful decorations, movement, and see this, you had to get that bus downtown. Howard Street, Lexington Street, and Charles Street to witness downtown shops and department stores.

The leading stores were Hutzler's, Hecht Co., Hochschild Kohn, and Stewarts. They all faced downtown Howard Street, 3 out of four, had side entrances on Lexington Street. Lexington Street connected to Charles Street. The location of the O'Neill's Department store. Downtown was the place to window shop, hopefully, make a purchase. That is where the saying window shopping started; that was a reality for some. In O'Neills during the 1930'st, the sales staff were primarily women; customers called them "misses," for Example, Miss Madeline. The "misses" would accompany a customer around their particular department and introduce items that might be of interest to the customer. And some customers wanted that service and depended on the sales lady's taste and judgment. Each saleslady or salesman knew their clientele and wore blue or black suits with white cuffs or collars. O'Neill's was a mid-Victorian style building with 35,000 feet of interior space. The store opened in 1882 and stood on the southwest corner of Charles and Lexington Streets and was the first store to come to mind, even though it closed in 1954. During my mother's teenage years, she worked in O'Neill's as a bundle wrapper (Gift wrappers). They wrapped the purchases with brown paper and a piece of string. The store was famous for its fine linens. My mother told the story that outside O'Neill's on the street corner stood a flower cart selling Gardenias with a straight pin so it would sit nicely on your dress or coat lapel. It was a very fashionable thing to do. The final look was so chic.

Thomas O'Neill was an Irish immigrant who had red hair and a red mustache. His portrait hung on the store's 1st floor, and he would greet his customers at the front door. This building escaped the great Baltimore fire in 1904, but not the modern times. Thomas O'Neill died in 1919; in his will, he ligated the Baltimore Archdiocese millions. Set aside monies for a new hospital. The Good Samaritan Hospital was completed and occupied in 1968. He was from the old way of thought to help the ones that helped you. He bequeathed the store to the workers in appreciation of their services, but in 1928, not even ten years later, it became the Hahn department store, but not for long change happened again. The building was demolished in January 1961 and had quite a sendoff. The farewell ceremony included a high school band playing Baltimore Our Baltimore, and Mayor J.H. Grady gave the signal for the 100-foot crane to launch its wrecking ball into the side of the building. Its site became the basics for One Charles Center, located at 100 North Charles Street. This building, considered international style, was constructed in 1962; its 23 stories of square Aluminum and glass. A new technique for Baltimore downtown. The keyword here is Square.

PHOTO COURTESY OF AAUBREY BODINE

One Charles Center

Since we were absent from a car, there was a particular type of clothing and accessories that were necessary.

Let's not forget the rain gear, since shopping those days required lots of walking, and the rain was sometimes a factor, so an umbrella, boots or goulashes. Yes, that is a word, and it means a type of rubber boot that's slipped over the shoes. There were different styles with different shapes of shoes they fit over a small high heel or had zippers in front for easy on and off. The older spelling of goulashes used in Great Britain and the locals. This chapter is not a department store history book but recollections of the downtown I knew. Madeline Vanik worked in several downtown department stores doing those years.

PHOTO COURTESY OF AAUBREY BODINE

Looking north from Howard Street and Fayette Street, you would have seen several Departments stores Hutzler's, Hochschild Kohn, Stewarts, and May company. Old photo 1948-1950

I had the opportunity to be there firsthand. These were sizeable and scenic stores in this section of Baltimore and now are gone. There was the excitement of getting on that bus at Fayette Street and Montford Avenue, heading downtown. Sometimes, I would meet my mother after her working day ended at Stewarts. The most important place for me was the toy department, especially the doll department. Yes, there was an area just for dolls. I loved the sparkle, lights, and dolls waiting for someone to own them. I wanted that to be me, sometimes daydreaming that I could get a doll that had hair and maybe a Comb. That came true; Christmas 1953, I received from Santa Mom. She put this Madame Alexander ballerina doll on lay-a-way. Christmas morning, she was sitting by the Christmas tree.

She is 18 inches long, wears a Toto, and has her comb. After waiting so long to have a doll with hair and I never touched the hair. I was thrilled with how she looked and wanted to keep her the same as when I saw her.

Here she sits still being the beautiful ballerina

Terri Lee doll, early 1950's sold at Stewarts

Stewart's and Company, this store opened in 1901 when Louis Stewart purchased Posner's Department store, located on the northeast corner of Howard and Lexington Avenue.

It was an ornate white Renaissance Revival building with roaring lions and beautiful wreaths, fluted columns with an open layout, large windows, and an excess of lights. Walking into this type of store was an eye-opening experience as a child. It seemed like I was amazed at almost everything. That's a good thing, and it sure kept me thinking. Still, now I feel an excitement for new sights and sounds. This particular store had a feeling of grandness different from the local shopping stores. Stewart's featured two restaurants: Georgian Tea Room and Cooks Works, and in 1931 was one of the first downtown stores to install air conditioning. But in 1979, Stewart's closed its doors forever. It was on the National Register of Historic Places in 1999.

COURTESY OF THE BALTIMORE MUSEUM OF INDUSTRY

Stewart and Company Lexington and Howard Street Year 1941

Hochschild Kohn toy delivery trucks 1920's/1930's

Hochschild Kohn's was originally a partnership between Max Hochschild, Bennie Kohn, and his brother Louis, in 1897, opened that year on the northwest corner of Howard and Lexington Streets. Paper shopping bags were available for a nickel, with the Hochschild Kohn logo. All the larger stores had their own. Madeline worked in the Pet Department that was on Lexington Street. This store was not as open and elegant as Stewart's and Hutzler's stores. Hochschild Kohn, like many downtown stores, had a Tea room with their specialties. It was a place where the shoppers got the whole experience, go up that fancy elevator, and go into a fancy dining room. The ladies would feel like they were a person of wealth or distinction, if only for a short period. The clinging of the dishes and teacups, happy voices, what a time that must have been. Madeline purchased a coat at Hochschild Kohn on the lay-a-way plan. It still is in beautiful condition.

1950's

This old Neo-Classical downtown store burnt in February 1983. The front of the building could not be saved, now there are no traces of the original structure.

COURTESY OF THE BALTIMORE MUSEUM OF INDUSTRY YEAR 1965

Hochschild Kohn Department Store and a busy downtown

The Atrium Apartments and Lofts replaced the -118 North Howard Street. Another square-cornered building with non-distinctive windows. Many new buildings that have replaced the old stores are not memorable.

This beautiful Romanesque décor was part of the Hutzler department store on Howard and Clay streets, next door to Hochschild Kohn's. To see the craftsmanship and pride that went into this back in the year 1888 is just astonishing. The Hutzler brothers wanted it to look like a palace hence the name Palace building. It started as a small dry goods store at Howard and Clay street by Abram Hutzler in 1835. The original Hutzler's opened in 1858 but burned down in 1888 and built the Palace. No more haggling over a price set by the store. They had a one-price policy, something new in the day. The entrance was two ornate doors with an ornamental entry and beautiful art deco. I can still remember pushing that large glass and metal-heavy revolving doors and getting a rush of fragrance.

Hutzler's was my favorite store. It was a beautiful place to walk around, especially in the fragrance and cosmetics department. Imagine seeing this beautiful stone entrance from the street, going thru the spotless rotating glass doors, with the wuss sound as the bottom rubbed on the marble floors. Now stepping on the landing that opened up to several steps down and looking out over bright, sparkling glass chandeliers and gleaming large glass bottles, glass countertops with flickering movement from the lights. It was like strolling thru another ecosphere. It was another fantasy sight for a young girl.

Here are examples of beautiful bottles from the cosmetic Department at Hutzler's.

I became acquainted with the store's dining areas by hearing my mother talk about the places she worked downtown. Hutzler's department store is one of them has four eating areas. The fancy one was on the 6th floor; the Colonial room was called the tea room. Equipped with mahogany tables and chairs, white linen tablecloths, and white cloth napkins. Toasted cheese bread, Chicken Chow Mein, and other specialties were on the menus. My Mother said something new was out Chicken Chow Mein she never heard of that before. Taste and traditions were changing and still are today. For dessert, there was the Wellesley fudge cake. I can just picture the Hutzler's Tea's room and nicely dressed ladies to be my Mom or one of her friends, maybe a neighbor. They wore their Sunday hats, nylons, heels, suits, or dresses just to come to the tea room and feel fancy. The attitude was to wear your Sunday best and look like a lady. The prices were quite affordable. On the 6th floor also was the Quixie opened just for lunch, but it did have a fancy dessert cart. Madeline would talk about the apple brown betty. The Quixie closed in 1972. There was also a basement luncheonette where most of the employees ate. Saratoga Potato chips with sandwiches named after Saratoga Street. Finally, there was a fountain shop located on Saratoga Street. Imagine those sounds of the old cash registers, people recounting their change, and the sounds of walking on the stone floors. All this together made you aware of where you were with all the smells, sounds, sights, and people of downtown. What a flat environment we live in today. These magnificent buildings and the shoppers are now a Tribute. Soon there was a new type of moving from floor to floor; it was called the escalator. Not sure when escalators came to downtown Baltimore. The escalators were created in 1899 by Otis Elevator Co., Charles Seeberger bought the patents, and the first installation happened in 1936. What a thrill was riding on this moving staircase, as they called it then. The elevators had elevator operators who would open the doors and close them manually. They verbally would call out down or up, name off the departments, lingerie, men's clothing, and others. The doors were always very ornate, as the stores were. Now escalators are commonplace. Here is an example of an older escalator mostly made of wood; when we would step down on the wood slots, they always felt wobbly. As a kid, it gave us a feeling of whether we would survive all this jolting, and we did. An imaginary adventure.

Other stores, like the Hecht Company, became the Hecht-May company in 1959, all located on Howard and Lexington streets.

The Virginia Dare store was a combination of restaurant, bakery, and candy store; it was another Downtown Howard Street must visit. My former classmate and friend Joanne worked in the candy area, which was in front of the store; she wore white gloves. My Mother would get the chocolate covered creams packaged by the store in a small white box with white doilies. The entrance floor was mosaic tile, an octagon shape of different blue shades, and a front door with a white wood frame. A large glass insert and a row of tall wood glass cases would sparkle with the lights hanging above them. It was a place that made you feel spirited. In the early sixties, it met its demise. But there are still

Below 1950's style and 1950 price

images in your memories of these charming places. I realize how lucky I was to have seen the exquisite sights of the past Howard Street. No photos can take the place of being there.

Many cities in our country do not care about preserving their heritage. Our children and the future world will never witness this. It's not essential to many people. Maybe they think it's old fashion. We must tell them that this did exist. No straight cold buildings, but works of art, that would make you ponder what our talented, artistic human counterparts accomplished long ago when life was a matter of how hard you worked to survive. It was a time of many changes politically, nationwide, and thoughts. It's a matter of humanoid pride that we review the past. Egypt had its pyramid, and Baltimore had Howard Street is enough for me. There was never a shortage of shopping in northeast Baltimore. We had many local stores and markets, areas that were accessible by walking. These areas were alive, stimulating, and filled with people. The lower-scale middle class was starting to grow. We were within walking distance to the Monument Street shopping area, our closer downtown, with no fancy doors and windows. My friend Terry, her sister, Jean, and I had a very memorable conversation and put this list of all the past businesses on Monument Street together. For history

Monument Pharmacy, Milton Avenue, and Monument street. Union Trust Bank, exotic Fur storage, Merelons card and gift shop, Lerner's, Sonya's Bridal Shop, Woolworths, Monumental five and dime, Princess Shops, Fongs Chinese Restaurant, Doll Shop, Logues Bike Shop, Art Shop, Petro Record Shop, Joe Marks Bar, Angelios Shoe Repair, Dan's Liquor Shop, Spill-Way Bowling Alley, Arundel Ice Cream, Webster Clothing, Levenson & Kliens Furniture, A & P Grocery Store, Irwin's Clothing, Johns Bargain stores, Pick & Pay, Liberace's Jewelry, White Coffee Pot, Little Tavern, Bares Hardware store, and Reads Drug Store. The area was dynamic and busy always thru all seasons. Our teen hangout on the corner of Monument and Bradford Street was the Arundel Ice cream store. Had a jute box on the back wall, nickel songs, booths in the back, cherry cokes, good friends, gossip, drama, familiar faces, and just good times. Angelio's Shoe Repair. When the soles or heels of your shoes wore down, you had your soles repaired or replaced. Even if your eyes closed, you would know that you just walked past the shoe repair shop, leather and shoe polish, what a great smell, not for everybody.

Nickey at Shoe Repair shop, East Monument Street

If you were a walker, this item was essential, the cart—1950' style.

When it comes to smells, the barbershop on Montfort Avenue, one block up from Monument Street, was the cleansing of your soul, the aroma of talc, shaving cream, and whatever else that great smell was. Before air-conditioning, the little shop doors would be open in the summer. You would hear the conversations and the aroma flow out the door, old city essence.

Stores like Monumental five & dime and Woolworths had essential merchandise and everyday stuff. The Art Shop, 2409 East Monument Street, sold painting supplies, books, cards, and children were not allowed without an adult; there is an Additional story about Art Shop in chapter 6.

If you needed bike repair or to purchase a new or used bicycle, there was Loque Bike Shop in 2527 East Monument Street near Montfort Avenue, opened initially by Mr. Logue's father, Bernard Logue Sr. This man was a wheelman pioneer and had some dealings with the Wright brothers. The store was a row house, and the family lived several doors down in a row house, and his shop area was on the first floor. It had a huge window, you could see inside, and Mr. Logue was working on those bikes. Most of these stores were no wider than 20 feet. Charlie Logue quit school in the ninth grade and worked for his Grandfather. Leaving school at a young age was a common thing to do in those days. Work and learning a trade were more critical than an ABC education. He was known by many people for his love of keeping the old bikes alive, his storefront window showed this old fashion bike with a large front wheel and a small rear wheel positioned high off the ground. Known as high wheelers. Every American Day Parade, he was on that bike, and everyone was amazed at how he could ride such a strange-looking object. Growing up near the bike shop and knowing some of the family gives me a sense of melancholy for Charlie Logue. He closed his business in 1989. He, like my mother, loved the neighborhood that once was, and when the time came to leave due to vandalism, drugs, and indifference. It was a sorrowful time for all involved.

Below is a picture of Bernard J (Boompy) Logue in front of his house on Monument Street with athe wooden bike that he made in the 1920s.

PHOTO COURTESY OF THE LOGUE FAMILY

One of the busiest places was Petro's Record Shop. You could order that particular 45 records that you heard on the radio the night before, and at that time, it was a music explosion. Every day came a new song. Rows of 45's records, single 78's, and albums had a dusty, old, plastic smell to the place. We wanted that music, labels like Argo, Herald, Old Town, Atlantic, Aladdin, RPM, Chex, Motown, Scepter, Coral, Whirling Disc, Chess, Federal, Mercury, Warner Brothers, Wee-Day, Dot, Red Robin, Ace, United Artist, Excello, Roulette, Specialty, Capitol, Bruce, Festival, Sound, Decca, Gee, Sun, Tag, Amazon, and more. Albums were becoming popular, including Johnny Mathis's album with songs like (Moonlight becomes you) and (Wonderful Wonderful). O Yeah. That was quite a memorable trip. Slow dancing. Read's Drug Store was the largest of neighborhood pharmacies, located on Chester and Monument Street, across the Northeast Market. On the upper floor was a balcony-type luncheonette. The steps were against the wall. You had a view of the downstairs; the small tables and chairs were at the edge of the balcony. It was a place to shop for personal items not available in the smaller drug stores or a tuna sandwich on toast and people watching. Down the street between Monument and McElderry street was little Chester Street, one entire block of everything. There was a public bathroom, a bar, furniture, an appliance store called Melikers, and Kohens shoe store that sold Buster Brown shoes, and I am saving the best for last. The Notions/sewing store was a kaleidoscope of colors; walking in that front door was an adventure for the senses. There were dozens of pattern cabinets, netting, and different shades and colors of the fabric roll, all tightly leaning on each other. Like many stores in those days, the floors looked old with openings in the wood and squeaked while walking on them. As you went in, the basement entrance was several feet straight ahead. After stepping down on the basement floor and looking forward, the sight was drawers of threads, all colors, patches, and buttons on small cards by the hundreds. Glass cases filled with novelties, who knows what else, it was packed. Smells that lingered with you of oldness, wood, and dust.

More shopping a little further away on the Avenue, short for Eastern Avenue. At 3818 Eastern Avenue was Epstein's Department Store, walk through the front entrance straight to the back entrance, thru the alley, and into the other part of Epstein's; the linens were in the back store.

In 1879, two brothers from Lithuania, Sidney and Samuel Epstein, after saving their money and working as clerks in other stores, decided to go for it and have their store. They opened and thrived for years on Eastern Avenue. They had the old-fashioned way of shopping, tiny racks with hangers, mostly tables spread out on the floor with the price tacked on the side. There were no frills or fancy doors. The primarily female employees at that time not only had to be available to help customers but also had other jobs during their day. There was sweeping the floor; the employees were the cleaning staff and layout the merchandise and whatever was necessary to keep the store up and ready. This store is the last family-owned and operated a department store in Baltimore. The store was closed in January 1991. The end of another era in Baltimore retail.

COURTESY OF THE BALTIMORE MUSEUM OF INDUSTRY

Eastern Avenue shopping area Year 1954

Now there is a new way of purchasing merchandise. We now have Amazon, eBay, and many other internet sites. Just sit in their chair and push the buttons. Please give me an open the door to walk thru and have an experience of old-fashioned shopping. Feeling the fabric, seeing the actual color, does it fit, and mostly have that sight and enjoyment of intermingling with people. Spencer's was the one clothing store for all the guys and the latest styles, for all their fancy threads, button suits, skinny ties, small collar shirts, and the latest shoes. It was across the street from Epstein's Department store on Eastern Avenue.

The picture shows the latest guy styles, those three-button suits,
skinny-tie, and button-down collars from Spencers

Left to the right: David S 500 block Port street, Irwin W 2400 block Jefferson Street Richard Vanik 408 North Port street, middle below Janet Vanik 408 North Port street: the picture taken in 1961. Easter in front of Jefferson Pharmacy, Montford Avenue, and Jefferson St.

There was McCrory's, other five and dimes, Buddies Men Shop, Spencer's Men Shop, several bars, Jewelry store, Santoni's grocery store, Yeager's music, card shops, restaurants, one with the best shrimp salad sandwiches around. There was always Lots of traffic, a profusion of sounds, and people being people. Perfect.

Soon we had a new guy in town, the Eastpoint Mall; we would grab the bus and check it out. There was locally a Robert Halls, E.J. Korvettes, Two Guys, and Pick and Pay. The neighborhood had the local delivery boys from our local corner grocery store. The door-to-door salespeople sell Wearever pots and pans (made in U.SA.) and go on a monthly payment plan. The salesmen would come to our homes for the collection of payments. Insurance salespeople, Photographers, Fuller brush, and cleaning products salesmen. Even politicians would come to the neighborhood asking if anyone needed a ride to the polls. It was never dull. All the salespeople were men; no women had those positions during the times. But there was a terrific movement of life. Ending this part of past Baltimore shopping experiences, we cannot forget that in 1816 there was a dollar store on West Lexington Street. The difference was instead of one dollar; it was one cent. What goes around comes around.

Chapter Eleven

HOLIDAYS

How lucky we are to have memories that satisfy our soul
In the times of darkness, we can descend on our life's
reflections
Just a spark can help you bring it together
Our feelings, beliefs, and inspirations will always fight
our desolation

Janet Divel nee Vanik 2017

The Holidays, especially Christmas, were a pure joy; it made everything else seem naught. The neighborhood and the local stores came alive with decorations, lights on the street wires, and street poles. Woolworth's five and dime stores were rustic, looking not fancy but familiar. There were wooden floors with large cracks and counters made of worn down brown wood, every time you took a step, there was a creaking sound as if the floor was telling us its old. Open and glass-covered cases invited us to take a look at Christmas, which was my favorite time of the year. First on the do list was to visit F. W. Woolworths was always a happy feeling walking into that store full of cheery sounds. There was a large bell hanging on the side of the old heavy door; I can still hear that clanging tone and heavy foot traffic sounds.

Christmas shoppers walked past a tradition at the Stewart Department store, windows displays. Notice the headgear of the day (head scarfs tied at the chin (babushka). Howard Street Year 1960

COURTESY OF THE BALTIMORE MUSEUM OF INDUSTRY

Christmas tea party with friends Kitty P and Janet V at East Jefferson Street Year 1950

Christmas garden figurines from Woolworth's, prices
varied from 2 cents to 25 cents 1950s

They sold silver tinsel wrapped in a single paper wrapper. Nothing went to waste those days; those loose little pieces of tinsel lying on the floor and out front of the store were a good find. We put them to good use on our Christmas tree. In the 1940s, my Grandmother Elizabeth would decorate her tree; it was a fake tree looking a little like Charlie Browns with homemade paper ornaments and cloth wire lined lights; a little tinsel brought it to life. One small box of decorations for the tree and a little sparkly tinsel satisfied us. My brother and I bought a real tree that one Christmas at the corner of the Red Wing theatre, we were both working part-time. Richard had a paper route, and I walked a younger student to school. We were very proud, mainly because our Mom smiled when we carried it into the house. The house finally smelled like a real Christmas tree, one of my dreams.

Tinsel Brilliance

After the passing of my grandmother, we retired her tree. It is in the old Christmas tree of heaven.

Original homemade ornaments 1940's / from the early 1950s.

The famous Grandmother tree, Port Street 1959,
and Deborah A enjoying the moment

One of the unique places to visit during Christmas was the Doll Shop, located on Monument Street, doll heaven for the girls, models, and trains for the boys. Every Christmas, they would put out a 4-page flyer, and that was the wish book for several weeks before Christmas, and most of the time, that was all. It was a wish. But it kept us optimistic.

Some Christmases, my brothers would be surprised with model airplanes. Many nights my brothers and I would create a plane, glue, and paint when available if you were lucky. Our favorite was the Mustang.

Hot items for boys: airplane models

Dick Tracy cap gun

Street Skates are well-liked by boys and girls. It was indeed a spectacular Christmas if skates were under the tree. They were our bike that was too expensive. We had to replace the wheels quite often. Concrete and asphalt wore that metal down. We sure could pick up speed, skating on the streets and alleys. This sport was for kids who were not afraid of getting scratched up. We needed to know how to stop. There were many broken bones for daring beginners. I only broke my hand and wrist once each. No brakes, helmets, gloves, or knee pads are available. Adrenaline-charged experience of the 1950s.

At that time, toys were separated by gender, which is how it was. A popular toy for boys were trains. Sometimes their sisters loved them too.

Christmas gardens were prevalent; they included a set of trains and tracks. Tiny plastic houses, plywood, and imagination. In the neighborhood, there were several houses people would open their doors to the neighbors, go down to their basement, and enjoy their creations. The train would be chugging and choo-chooing around the tracks. Some of the engines blew smoke. Tiny lights in the houses make believe snow, mirrors for ponds with ice skaters doing their thing, maybe a farmhouse and some pigs, sheep, and horses. But the train was the attention-getter and the little red caboose.

Plastic buildings for the Christmas garden

COURTESY OF ALAMY

This is one of my favorite images of our vanishing world. It feels like it could have been Monument Street. The decorations and lights hung across the streets, snow-filled payments trampled down by footprints, ladies in long coats, dresses, heels, and nylons feeling that cold. Use umbrellas to try to keep dry. It is just a perfect photo of the 1950s in the city at Christmas.

Remembering Monument Street at Christmas is probably one of the most loving memories with the sights, sounds, sights, and people. Now, I know, knowing nothing will ever be like that again. The churches got into the spirit by singing carols at church service. Every year St. Elizabeth would give out food boxes, and there would be one on our front steps. My favorite Christmas song was Silver Bells; the keyword here is the city. Silver Bells It's Christmas time in the city; ring-a-ling, ding-a-ling, soon it will be Christmas Eve. Remembering that cold crisp air and wishing I didn't forget my gloves. Walking in that snowy slosh, feeling the crunch with snowflakes landing on my face, sometimes tasting one or two, sounds of Salvation Army bells ringing, hanging lights reflecting on the snowy pavement, Christmas music, people with a purpose, looking like penguins, all bundled up. Real Christmas trees and wreaths for sale on the corners, with beautiful smells and sounds.

Downtown was another special place, grabbing that 23 bus in the evening or weekend and seeing the upper-scale Christmas decorations. They were at the large department stores on Howard Street. The window displays were glorious to any child and probably to some adults who still had that child in their hearts. Bright lights with animated-mechanical elves, bears, choir boys, bugle boys, dancers, reindeer, Christmas carols, and of course, Santa. Some of the characters talked, laughed, and had music box sounds. What more could we ask for just a little imagination? What a great culture at that time. Christmas meant other things like events and the excitement of seeing what the holiday could bring to a child with wide eyes. I talked about the department stores and other landmarks that are no longer with us and are now just a distance visual memory. One place that still exists is the nineteenth-century opulence Hippodrome Theatre, which seated 3,000 people, and in the 1930's it was in decline, but In 1931 L. Edward Goldman purchased the theatre for $14,000. The theatre saw a new birth under management. Eventually, Isidor Rappaport brought the theatre up to date with a new marquee and new seats and brought in celebrities, such as Jack Benny, Bob Hope, Frank Sinatra, and others. The Hippodrome had its final live vaudeville show in 1959, and due to television, where people could see live shows in the comfort of their own homes, the Hippodrome closed its doors in 1990. The France-Merrick Performing Arts Center purchased it in 2004 and is now a functioning multipurpose center. Beautiful still

PHOTO COURTESY OF RON LEGLER INTERIOR

From 1951-to 1953, the Hippodrome sponsored Christmas shows for the city's underprivileged children. We received an invitation to the Christmas show, and of course, we went, took the bus on Fayette Street, and went downtown. I finally had a special occasion to wear my plaid jumper. I waited so long to wear this used but beautiful red pleated jumper, and you could do a spin. Little girls know what that is. Found the theatre thanks to Richard; he was a great navigator, me not so much. We always had disagreements about directions and where places were, and he always won. We arrived to see large crowds waiting in line when finally getting to the front doors. I thought it was a castle; I still believed in fairies at that time, which made it more magical. There were large glass front doors, carpet on the floors, and decorations on the walls, and again the thought came to me. I thought this honestly has to be a castle or was at another time. My imagination went wild. I wondered what the people looked like who lived there so long ago. There was a vast staircase, dimly lit, we went up to the balcony, and when all the lights came on, our eyeballs were getting splashed with new sights. Lots of red and round curved balconies? The people below us combined with movement noisy chatter, and then the stage lit up, and the show started. An enormous glass chandelier hung from the ceiling, and of course, there was that sparkle, and I became hypnotized. The singing and the dancing on the stage were just magic. At the show's end, the entertainers sang; I 'm dreaming of a white Christmas and invited the audience to sing along. It was an extraordinary time for many kids, and I never dreamed of seeing this. Every time I hear White Christmas, I think of that day. After the show, we all stood in line to receive a gift, given in alphabetic order. The girls would receive a doll and the boys a car or a truck. Since my last name was Vanik, we were at the end of the line, and by the time I got there, no more white baby dolls. I received my doll. She is a six-inch plastic black baby doll. I was surprised but took her home, and she became part of my doll family, called her Nellie. I still have her. Thanks to Richard, we got on the right bus and made it home ok. Meet Nellie

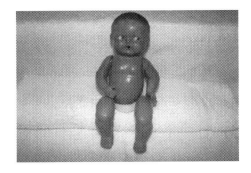

Celebrated In the 1940s and 1950's still the old European customs. There was Saint Wenceslaus, Saint Nickolas, and Christmas day mass. We heard carols like O Tannenbaum, which was an old German folk song that became associated with Christmas in the 19th century. The English-language phrase O Christmas Tree was first recorded in 1835 and represented a tradition from the German language. At St. Wenceslaus they were still using the old Czechoslovakian songbook for mass. When the older generations, mostly the immigrants, were no longer there, the old ways went in another direction. It developed more into Santa Claus instead of Saint Nickolas. He looked more up to date in his clothing, and of course, he laughed and did the Ho Ho Ho thing. St Nickolas was a stationary figure. Not as attractive in a store window. The essential items like socks, sweaters, and gloves were more in line with the budget; my mother, Madeline, was Santa Claus. Grandmother Elizabeth would supply the stockings with an orange, apple, nuts, and hard candies. To us, this was a treat, especially the nuts, mostly walnuts, and there was a unique nutcracker that only came out at Christmas.

One of the main dishes for Christmas time was oyster stew and oyster crackers, bread pudding with vanilla sauce, and maybe baked apples with cinnamon topping. My Grandmother made Sugar cookies only at Christmas time, which was my Grandmother's role. We would try to grab some of that raw cookie dough, but my grandmother was on to us. She would say something in German, like Dumkof, which pretty sure is not a flattering word. I especially remember the apron my Grandmother and Mother wore those days. It was only a piece of cloth, the size of a small bath towel, but it had extraordinary storage potential and a handy wash rag. It covered the housedress to protect it from everyday usage and baking.

The brownie and Girl Scout troops would go caroling around the neighborhood.

At Saint Wenceslaus auditorium, the Christmas movie was Toyland, the 1930s version. It was the same movie every year. It sounds old hat, but like many things, it was another small adventure in a little kids' life. I was amazed every time I saw it. At that time, getting ready for Christmas was more important, not all the gifts, but the cookies, the nuts, oyster stew, the Christmas tree, the lights, family, friends, and neighbors. People seemed happier; it was out of the norm and just that exciting feeling of a change in the air. I never realized that this was one of the most significant times of my life with my little family.

The music of Gene Autry singing Frosty the snowman and When Santa Claus gets your letter. There was Jimmy Boyd with I saw Mommy kissing Santa Clause, but as the '50s left, and the 60 came, and with my grandmother's passing, Christmas changed. The regular regiment, traditions, and the familiar smells and sounds were gone. Our habits and culture are now on the back shelf, and the present was here. But my Grandmother did leave her footprint on her descendants. As time went by, customs and habits changed to whatever we made them. Anyone can start their traditions. We can leave our footprint for our descendants. After all, we are their ancestors. I was lucky my stern German Grandmother left her spirit, even if it's just in my heart.

PHOTO COURTESY OF AAUBREY BODINE

Wishing is a human passion. Without that hope in your heart, what would tomorrow be?

Janet Divel nee Vanik 2017

Springtime and Easter

Easter 1947 A wonderful Easter for Joanne Dressel.
North Rose Street, a classmate, and best friends.

Easter bonnets, in the 1950s and early '60s, the
women's hats were tiny with netting.

Easter meant Parades, and Baltimore had their share of parades in every part of the city back then. There was a parade at Charles Street that started at the Washington Monument and slowly traveled down to the University parkway. There were parades in south Baltimore, at Eastern Avenue. Our neighborhood parade was on Monument Street, The retailers built a platform over the steps of a bank building on Collington Ave and Monument St., and all the dignitaries would sit and observe the Easter Parade. People would walk past and hope their hat gets noticed. Of course, the attraction was the Easter Bonnet

1950's fancy Easter bonnet

On parade day, there was an Easter Bonnets contest. By tradition, a fancy hat was a Christian head covering on Easter. It also represents the wearing of new clothes during Easter services at church. Today the Easter bonnet has graduated to a decorative accessory for the day. Things are piled on it, which creates a personal act of self-style. It's the modern version of a slowly disappearing tradition. The Saturday before Easter, it was everyone's responsibility to get their Mom a corsage, so on Easter morning, she would wear it on her coat to Easter mass.

Easter Janet and brother Richard 1948

Popular songs around that time were Here Comes Peter Cottontail, sung by Mervin Shiner and later 1957 by Gene Audrey. In our neighborhood, on Easter day, all the kids were bringing outside their Possible winning egg. The contest winner was whoever cracked their opponent's egg when hitting both ends; they would win the opponent's egg that broke. I have no idea where that game originated. But it was severe cut-throat moments going on. Hippity, hoppin, Easter 's here

Madeline and son Richard Outside St. Wenceslaus lot Easter 1965
style, Fancy: notice white gloves and still small netted hat.

Halloween was another celebration. On Monument Street, our local shopping area, they were a parade on Halloween night. Neighbors were all out in their pretend garb, mostly white sheets. Many ghosts were hovering around, bums, princesses, witches, anything to act out pretending to be something else. These costumes were never store-bought. That was not available then, all just put together with what was available, and it all worked out. One year, mid-fifties, I went dressed as a gypsy; my grandmother gave me an old embroidery blouse, my costume; I thought it looked pretty good. With my Mothers red lipstick, I was a gypsy. While walking among the ghost, there was all of a sudden this big white thing coming towards my face, and then the words "Makeup," one of my male classmates, James, had in his grubby paws a colossal powder puff, and he smacked it right at my face. I had a new look, maybe a gypsy ghost. People, movement, and laughter create a visual picture for my memory box. Trick or treat was tricky and not as popular as today. Many of the neighbors would turn off their lights and pretend not to be home or just would not answer the door. Of course, some of the kids created a trick for that one. Straight pins were the weapons; they could stick them into those

old-fashioned doorbells, then run and peak around the alley. Sooner or later, that door would open to remove the pin and wonder who the culprits were. The kid will be a kid.

The gypsy blouse. Handmade from Hungary and beautiful. Year possible early 1930's

Getting around the town

The main form of transportation was using our feet; walking was how we got around. As the years went by. I learned how to get a streetcar or a bus to get where I wanted to.

COURTESY OF ALAMY

Passengers on the bus at 4 pm, Baltimore Maryland Year 1943. Pullstring above windows for letting the bus driver knows you are getting off the bus.

For years yellow was the color of all the old buses and streetcars. Most of the families in my neighborhood did not own a car in the 1940s and '50s. The streetcars, also called trolleys, ran on rails. Iremember my mother taking my brothers and me on the streetcar out to Belair Road, a suburb of Baltimore city, to our grandparent's house on Necker Avenue. That trip started on a streetcar, then a transfer to another streetcar, finally getting picked up at a red brick building, the Bus Depot. The streetcars were noisy, metal on metal, squeaking, clanging, rocking back and forth, and the burned smell after the sparks flew on the wires. Every time I rode the streetcar, I got motion sickness. We were taking our lives into our hands, leaving the vehicle. Sometimes the rails were in the middle of the street. There were no pavements (sidewalks), and the streetcar followed the tracks. We were ultimately in the middle of the street with traffic on both sides. There was a very functional light rail system from the city to the adjoining counties for 104 years before the buses finally won on November 3, 1963. The streetcar tracks were a real problem for bike riders, cars, pedestrians, high heels, and roller skaters. Most of the tracks were removed. The old cobblestone streets still show evidence of being paved over with asphalt. Overhead wires, yellow streetcar and buses, asphalt, rails, cobblestones, traffic, and people are stirring, brown-bagging lunch. The maze of overhead wires and rails was a part of Baltimore City, a significant change with them gone.

COURTESY OF BALTIMORE MUSEUM OF INDUSTRY YEAR 1954

Eastern Avenue and Conkling Street

The routes followed the original streetcars, from the 1890s thru the 1960s, operated by the Baltimore Transit company, the streetcar's demise took place between 1947 and 1963. With its rails demolished, Baltimore was no longer a streetcar city.

A little history about the streetcars in Baltimore, it was the first city to have commercial operated Streetcars. They started running on August 10, 1885. It replaced horse-drawn cars. The original technology at that time was that the middle rail had the current use as its power supply. A newer streetcar system was installed in 1891, using underground steel cables to pull the cars. That system did not work too well in 1899. Finally, after years of trying this and that, overhead lines were throughout the city and its suburbs. Something new, a new coal-burning power plant, was built on Pratt Street. In the same area, there were four 190-foot smokestacks installed. Welcome to a street-car city and lots of pollution till 1963. The city converted to all rubber tire buses after the streetcar's demise. Streetcars and buses took us to Gwynn Oak and Carlin's amusement Parks, downtown, work, shopping, visiting, roller skating rinks, dances, entertainment, restaurants, Doctors, schools, new hangouts, and just about anywhere else any distance from your neighborhood.

Young couple at East Fayette Street and North Lakewood Avenue, in the shadow of The Hiker statue. A Spanish American War Memorial dedicated on June 11, 1943, this 9-foot granite base-depicting a soldier clad in a period uniform with a campaign hat and a Krag Jorgensen rifle.

Transit bus with rubber tires, number 23 bus in right side background. The bus for downtown and Sparrows point/ Shipyard.

The year 1954

In the new era, the Metro Subway opened in 1983, and the new rail system in 1992.

Light rail opening 1992 on Howard Street year 2017. It's a new way of transportation, but it sure looks familiar. I have seen this before; they look like overhead wires and tracks. What goes around comes around.

Chapter Twelve

JUST BECAUSE IT
HAPPENED – RIPPLES

Some events create ripples and expand to a force of change and affect us all. Most of the families who lived in the neighborhood were descendants of European immigrants who came to America in the early years, creating quite a ripple.

During the 1940s thru the 1950's Baltimore was booming with opportunities for anyone looking for a job, not necessarily the job we wanted, but something to pay the bills. New veteran's benefits came into being. What pushed this boom was the increase in military producing factories during that time There were two major wars. Made in the USA was the motto. Dependable employers were Sparrows Point Steel Mill, Fairfield Shipyard, GM, Western Electric, National Brewery, Hamm's Beer, American Brewery, Dr. Pepper, London Fog coats, Calvert Distillery, National Can, Rice's Bakery, McCormick Spice, Pompeian Olive Oil, Mitchell Corn, Muskin Shoe Company, Bata Shoe Factory, Sinclair Oil Company, Continental Can Co., Crosse and Blackwell, Esskay Meat Packing, Stieff Company, Koppers Steel, Sewing factories, S & H Stamps, American Oil Co., Domino Sugar, downtown stores, small business, and many more no longer existed in the city. Another big ripple happened when the companies that rose out of the American Cities decided that more money was to be made for their shareholders by out Sourcing to other Countries. It was an abandonment of the city. Made-in America companies were deserting their own country and workers. Those smaller companies gave Baltimoreans a decent life, the beginning of the middle class. When the jobs disappeared, it was the beginning of hardships for many people, especially in the city. Most of the people on my side of town did not go or finish high school. College was a dream unless we could support ourselves while attending school, with no freebies.

The times were changing. There started to be two-income families. The neighborhood comfort was dissolving right before our eyes. The change was here. There was this question, Now What? Baltimoreans are resilient in a daunting time, but this left a scar. As I mentioned before, when the large exit happened in the 60s and 70s, it changed everything as far as our way of living and the culture disappeared. It was desertion of our city's history. The immigrants started the ripple thru hard work, and sadly, the waves getting thinner were spreading out of the city.

October 1961, Sinclair Refining Company, in the mid-sixties the company was bought out by British Petroleum. Located in the Curtis Bay area. This picture consists of Janet (5th from the right) and the lady's office workers.

An example of the every two-week paycheck back in 1961, Federal insurance is now known as Social Security. Transportation to and from work meant: walk, bus, transfer to another bus, walk.

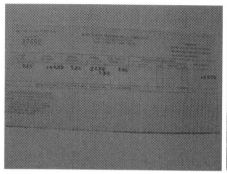

COURTESY OF BALTIMORE MUSEUM OF INDUSTRY

Esskay Meats 3800 East Baltimore Street 1940's

There were many joyful moments throughout those years. For one, the year 1951 thru 1952 on Saturday mornings, a children's TV program filled with fireflies, characters like talking horses, Charlemane the lion, evil spider-lady, Heathcliff the horse, flannel mouse, and a whistling wizard. It was a story about an ordinary boy, J.P., who unexpectedly finds himself in a fantastic world. This place was called "Land of Beyond," and J.P. happily explored to find the Whistling Wizard and there were many adventures to be had. This show was very much ahead of its time, created by Bill and Cora Baird, and brought humor about the humdrum world. This show was the first of its kind to be broadcast in Technicolor. The Bairds were premiere puppeteers of the '50s. But as things were those days, CBS thought that their techniques were too expensive, too out there, and after one season, canceled the show. When the show was on a local Baltimore channel, I was lucky to see it at a neighbor's house. There was a drawing contest, and at ten years old, I entered with a postcard. To my wonderful surprise, I received this letter and have cherished it ever since.

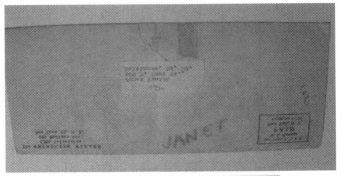

The year 1951

Now, let us go straight to strip clubs, quite a different subject. In 1955 there was street education as well. Sometimes sitting on those Baltimore steps at night, people would get these outrageous ideas, and some would fall for them. I was a member of the younger bunch and susceptible to those who were maybe mature. Several blocks away, down on 3821 Pulaski Hwy. (straight down Orleans Street) was located at the Sherries Show bar, a strip club. It looked like a dark hole like the places on Baltimore Street. A plan was that everybody was going to the Sherries Show Bar; my friends and I were 14 years old. There were eight people; we all had coats on; it was frigid that night. The older group was the shields.

The trick was getting the younger and smaller ones without the bouncer spotting us. We were encircled by the oversized coats; a quick push into the door. It felt like we were robbing a bank, and this was the getaway; instead, we were trying to get in. We went into almost complete darkness, and there was a dim light above the stage. But I remember the whole incident, how could I forget an adventure like this, as we walked in, to the right are steps maybe two and three, stepping up to large booths against the wall, we rushed and sat down toward the corner, the older ones were on outside of us. Quickly, the curtain opened, and on the stage appeared this woman with fake fur wrapped around her, twirling around the stage. She started releasing herself of all that heavy clothing. It was down to a tiny piece of material on her body, which left nothing to the imagination. The music got louder, and she was dancing and meandering around the stage. She grabbed two foxtails and started her foxtail dance, which included moving them from her neck area to between her legs. Making weird motions. The lights turned down near the end of that performance, and It was time to leave. We did the same formation leaving and escaping; it felt relieved getting outside. It was quite an experience; the logic of it, if any, was just another neighborhood adventure, and we grew up faster seeing the different sides of life. What mattered was how we perceived the information. Every time I passed that place

after our visit, it brought back that cold night and amity bond in our neighborhood. There was not a moment that night that I felt fear or was not protected. What a great thing to feel. Not all ripples were as exciting and esteemed. Times got dark just as there was brightness; it had to be the other side, too; that's life. When I was a young child, I wanted fantasy and fairies to be real and enjoy what I thought was happiness forever, but instead, it got real. But the fairy tale belief did not last.

My real-world brandished one day in the year 1952. A visit to the Red Wing theatre with two friends was the beginning of my other side of life. While sitting in the seat, suddenly, this strange man with long wild hair sat next to me and asked if I wanted some candy; I tried to ignore him. His face was touching the side of mine; he started to fondle me. Frightened, I moved to the other side, which was a foolish thing to do, but I was young at age 11 and could not figure out what was happening. I was bewildered. Who is this man? What is he doing?. He moved next to my friend and started to do the same thing to her. We panicked and ran out of the theatre. My friend told her Mom what happened, and she called the police. They came to our house and asked questions. The man was still in the theatre and arrested. The trial was in the courthouse downtown; the Judge took us to his chambers because of our age. Walking into that building felt like going into a vast void. Voices would echo off the walls, and when I walked into the main room, I felt like everyone was watching us. I just zoned it out. Lucky for us, the judge settled this in his chambers.

The man was charged with sexual assault and received prison time. There was no counseling or Doctor checkup during that time; you had to toughen up. For a while, I felt he was always there, in the area, or with someone who looked like him. I would duck down the alley to avoid any contact. But in time, we all went on, just a lousy ripple.

We heard of many folklores; one was a myth called Black Aggie, a statue of great mystery, not knowing if she had any influence on us, earthly teenagers. She was the tomb decoration on the grave in 1925 of General Felix Agnus in Druid Ridge Cemetery in Pikesville, Maryland, is an unauthorized replica of an 1891 symbolic figure called Grief. General Agnus had reproduced from an original by the artist Augustus St. Gardens.

This strange figure's story has many turns; for years, everyone heard of that statue in the cemetery. One afternoon in 1955, I and several friends, one with a car, put all our change together for gas and decided to visit this far away, spooky place and see for ourselves. As the sun went down and we were staring at Black Aggie, it did not take long for us girls to decide to leave. OK, we saw it now, let's go, but the guys had other plans. Why not leave the girls here and drive away? Ha Ha. Ripples that is what they made, sheer horror. Here we were staring at a cold gray hooded face partly visible and could declare if it was dead or alive. Apparently, with heavy hearts, the guys drove back to rescue us. That statue had a ghostly feel about it. In the 1960s, vandalism was getting so bad that the descendants of Agnus decided to donate Black Aggie, and on March 18, 1967, Black Aggie went to the Smithsonian Institute for display. For many years Black Aggie was missing; she was not on any records stating where she was. She was at the National Museum of American Art in storage for many more years. In 1996 a young Baltimore writer did a story on Black Aggie and raised her from the dead by locating her. Today Aggie sits at the Federal Courts building in Washington DC, in the rear courtyard of the Dolly Madison house. How sad that some people cannot respect someone's final resting place and statue. But she was saved.

In the mid-1950s, the Ringling Bros. and Barnum & Bailey Circus came to Town, and elephants were walking down Pulaski Highway to get to the armory. They called it The greatest show on earth in the 18th and 19th centuries. In Baltimore, that venue was at the Fifth Regiment Armory on North Howard and West Preston streets. The Shiners sponsored the circus show that my brothers and I attended. TheShriners is an organization with members being Master Masons in the Freemasonry Fraternity and others. I remember people going around during the show selling little lizards/anoles; green in color attached around their neck was a string and a safety pin. People would wear them. How bizarre! I'm sure the anoles had a short life span.

PHOTO COURTESY OF AAUBREY BODINE

Baltimore Harbor looking north, 1955

The Mathison Building, on the left side of the photo, was one of the most iconic art deco skyscrapers in Baltimore. It is 34 stories tall and has been the tallest building for 44 years. This red brick and limestone exterior with its gold crowned tower inlaid with 24-carat gold leaf by Henry Miller in 1929. The lobby, along with its elaborate elevator doors, has 45 foot richly carved wood ceilings, Greco-Roman-style columns and inlaid mosaic floors. The exterior carvings around the doors illustrate the great fire of Baltimore 1904, writings from the 'Star-Spangled Banner," and, of course, a little of Baltimore-style bronze window grates decorated with crabs. Located at 10 Light Street, corner of Light Street and Redwood street. From 1957 till 1958, at the age of sixteen, I worked for the Fidelity-Baltimore National Bank in the Mathison Building worked on the 4th floor and operated a bin sorting machine. There were rows of large bins with a chair facing the bins and a keyboard. The operator would deposit checks into the correct slot. A filing system, as the container turned to each space, would make a loud vrrrrrrrrrrrrrrm sound. No earplugs for that very noisy job.

Various methods of thought raised many young girls at that time. The main one was for us to get a husband, have babies, and sort out the rest later. There were many walls and some too tough to climb, especially for disadvantaged women and girls who felt this. The three indicators of this plight were poverty, under-educated equaled submission. It did not matter what nationality or race you were: the idea was there. I realized at a young age, at least the thought was there, that I might be that lady in the housedress and usually an apron to top off the look, and I did not want to be that lady. But like so many other girls at that time, I found myself in that world of young love and expecting Shangri-La. But as life would have it, that's not what I got. We knew if you make a mistake in life, you have to fix it. Sometimes we have to tell a story that might embarrass us. Maybe make you appear to be several different people throughout your lifetime. Now at a much later time, I ask myself how and why did I get myself in that position. Time has a way of questioning and getting to understanding those questions. At seventeen and working a full-time job, I became pregnant, this was a frightful, confusing time, and I felt very alone. No basic healthcare safety at that time. I became a wife at seventeen and the mother of a beautiful baby girl. I believe it had to do with how your reputation looked in many decisions those days. Time went by. I worked hard to get my life in order. I did not want to get into that cycle. So, at the first opportunity, I obtained a divorce. Taking on the responsibility of my child was what I did. I had dreams, But in my situation, during those times, I could not get past the no-option button. I never had an understanding of who I was and my worth. In today's world, things are changing, which is excellent.

Women's jobs were primarily sales ladies, waitresses, barmaids, saloon entertainers, house cleaners, clerks, secretaries, and factory workers.

There were more ripples ongoing. Birth control was a sin in the Catholic Church. The alternatives for unwanted pregnancies were illegal abortion, self-abortion, or adoption thru the Church. They would send the girl to an unmarried girl's home, have the baby, and take care of the adoption. After that awful experience, the girls were now a strain and an embarrassment for her family. It is a fact that many girls in later life felt tremendous guilt in giving up their babies. If their family disowned them, they would be out on the street, and if the baby's father did not want to marry her, it was tough luck. I kept moving forward: when the combination of lack of self-respect, constant anxiety, and mix that with poverty, you have an assault on your person. I could not see myself out of that life. But I did. I guess I did get some of my dreams.

Those days are gone. Education is the key to ending this. But I have to remember that with misfortune, ripples were also the good old days. Including my neighborhood was my lift to my inter being and having each other for a time. Some of us survived. I want to think it was the determination we had to do better or maybe sheer luck. My real-life education was far from over; there were plenty of lessons left to learn and many more experiences in East Baltimore.

Several blocks down from the Mathison Building on Baltimore and Redwood Street was an area much different from most of the city. (The Block) located on the 400 blocks of Baltimore Street. The block is where not too many people would take a walk thru their lunchtime. Being on the curious side, I did just that. Many open doors, loud music, shouting from inside and outside the buildings, dirty payments with cigarette butts, and old flyers were lying in the smelly gutters. The aroma of cigarette smoke, ashtrays, liquor, and who knew knows what else, with men saying things I did not care to hear. I got out of there unscathed but a little more knowledgeable about what was going on there. In the earlier days, it was famous for its burlesque houses. In the 1950s, the clubs became sleazy. Strip clubs and sex shops replaced the old business. Several films featured this area. Liberty Heights and Diner, and in an independent feature, On the Block.

COURTESY OF MARYLAND CENTER FOR HISTORY AND CULTURE

Gayety nightclub year 1953 The Block

The passing decades would see a shrinking of this area. Once several blocks long, stretching almost to Charles Street in the central part of downtown, the Block is now about two blocks long from South street to Gay street. There was the Gayety, not a Saturday afternoon movie theater, more famous for strippers. Another time in the past.

On a lighter note, as a child, I remember our radio was constantly blasting with the Colts or Orioles games. Baseball and football were my brother's objects of affection. I should throw in Wrestling, crazy stuff.

In 1953 the Baltimore Colts were established in Baltimore City and had their games at Memorial Stadium on 33rd Street during their entire tenure in Baltimore. During the 1950s and 1960s Baltimoreans enjoyed mainly having a winning team, and the fans are die-hards. The Colts won their first NFL Championship in 1958. That NFL Championship game is widely known as the "Greatest Game Ever Played" for its dramatic conclusion with quarterback Johnny Unitas marching the Colts downfield in sudden death overtime and Alan Ameche scoring the winning touchdown on a 1-yard run. Much of the credit for Baltimore's success went to Hall of Famers Johnny Unitas, halfback Lenny Moore and wide receiver Raymond Berry.

When it came to Baltimore sports, the end for many fans came when the Baltimore Colts became the Indianapolis Colts. The move to Indianapolis happened on March 29, 1984, in the middle of the night. The city of Indianapolis made an offer for the Colts franchise to move there. Baltimore was unsuccessful at persuading them to stay, so the city government attempted to get the state legislature to condemn the Colts franchise and give ownership to another group that would promise to keep the Colts in Baltimore. Under the threat of eminent domain from the city of Baltimore, the franchise relocated to Indianapolis. Everyone who was a fan felt abandoned. My older brother Bob passed before that happened, he could not participate in sports, but he made up for it with his knowledge and loved souvenirs. He was homebound. His favorite souvenir was a 1954 Oriole baseball; he received it in 1954. This ball always had a front-row seat on Bobby's table.

The 1954 Baltimore Orioles baseball and case

During the 1950'5 and 1960, the Memorial Stadium was the place to go for the Orioles or the Colts. It was at 900 East 33rd Street. This rebuilt multi-sport stadium was reconstructed with an upper deck and completed in the summer of 1954 and was named the Memorial Stadium or, as some called it, The old gray lady of 33rd Street. It was closed in 1997 and demolished in 2002. There now stands a YMCA and an apartment complex.

Other Baltimore news was about the possibility of a bridge crossing the Chesapeake Bay started in 1880. The first known proposal to build this bridge came about 1907/1908 and called for a crossing between Baltimore and Tolcheater Beach. There were plans in 1927 for the new bridge. Following the stock market crash of 1929, the construction of a Baltimore to Tolchester Beach crossed with the American economy's collapse resulting in the Great Depression of the 1930s. Ferries were the primary transportation mode across the bay from the colonial period until completing the 1952 bridge. The eastbound lane opened on July 30, 1952, and the westbound opened on June 28, 1973. The original span opened in 1952 and, with a length of 4.3 miles, was the world's longest continuous over-water steel structure. William Preston was the 52nd Governor of Maryland, initiated its construction in the late 1940s. This bridge is unique; it has three identifying names known "Bay Bridge," Maryland Bay Bridge" and America's Scariest Bridge" because of its height and the narrowness of the spans. This bridge has no soft shoulders and low guardrails, an elevation of 22,790 feet, and the narrowness of the spans. One thousand six hundred feet and add high winds, vehicles, especially tractor-trailer trucks, might have a problem. It is significant-time scary. The completion of this bridge between Kent Island and the western shore in 1954 changed the eastern shore. Bay Bridge Rising

PHOTO COURTESY OF AAUBREY BODINE

Back in the day, this Baltimore area was the exit point for the city vacationers to go to the seashore, beaches, and amusement parks. The Bay Bridge in 1952 changed the Eastern shore of Maryland and ended an era of something that will never be seen again crossing that water, Steam Boats.

PHOTO COURTESY OF AAUBREY BODINE

ROUNDTRIP—Value $1.25

This section good for
return trip from
Tolchester Beach to Baltimore
aboard the

S. S. TOLCHESTER

Good Any Regular Trip During 1953
And Must Be Detached At Boat

This section good for outgoing
trip to Tolchester Beach from
Baltimore

S. S. TOLCHESTER
Pier 5, Pratt Street
Subject to Government Tax
Good Any Regular Trip During 1953
And Must Be Detached At Boat

Steam Ship Bay Belle 1950s

The names that come to mind were Betterton Beach and Tolchester Beach, located on the eastern shore. Kent Island. People in the city were trying to get some relief from the summer heat, to get to Tolchester or Betterton would first have to board a steamboat " Bay Belle" or S.S. Tolchester at the pier 15 on Light street, or pier five at Pratt street, then travel 27 miles across the bay. Tolchester had an amusement park, hotels, and other entertainment. Fewer vacationers came during the Depression and World War 11 and when the bridge in 1952 opened, it allowed people to drive across the Chesapeake from the western shore over to Ocean City in the 1950s. Tolchester Beach fell into decline, and in 1962 was sold. Also, Betterton Beach was a thriving vacation spot for the city's people. At that time, most people did not have an automobile for personal use, so getting the bus down to the piers was their way of vacation, even if it was for one day. Some people would get a two-way ticket and return the same day. Betterton followed Tolchester Beach and fell in disarray; with the hotels gone, all the old landmarks were gone. In 1978 Kent county purchased much of the old resort property to create a public beach. In the early 1950s, my Mom took my brothers and me on that steamboat across the Chesapeake Bay to visit Betterton Beach. An incredible experience to walk up a gangplank up to this enormous boat. When the ship left the pier, the wind sounded annoyed. The sounds were mostly fog horns blowing and the continuous sound of engines turning. A new experience, nothing like city traffic. I stood alert on the deck until I could adjust to this strange new world; this new feeling was one of openness and lots of water. We survived that 27-mile bouncy trip with a packed lunch, tuna fish sandwiches on white bread, and some olives in a jar, and on the return trip, dinner was tuna fish sandwiches on white bread, no olives. Things were good, except for the sand in my pants. There were no thermal coolers available, and the metal picnic basket held the lunch/dinner. The sights and sounds have certainly changed; what a remembrance.

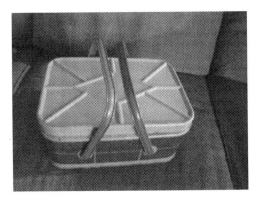

original lunch basket

Our city living allowed neighborhood kids to get together and take the bus or #32 streetcar to Gwynn Oak Amusement Park. During those days, there were three parks Gwynn Oak, Carlins, and Bay Shore, they were our Disneyland, Kings Dominion, and Great Adventure, only on a much smaller scale. During the 1950's Gwynn Oak had three partially wooden roller coasters. Notice the word wood, the Big Dipper, Little Dipper, the Wild Mouse, Ferris wheel, merry-go-round, and my favorite, the Whip. The rides were on the old side, but we got the excitement we were looking for and, at that time, a safe place to go. Similar rides were at Carlins Park with the wooden roller coaster. The only safety feature was the front bar; forget seat belts, hold on.

PHOTO COURTESY OF AAUBREY BODINE

Carlins Park wooden roller coaster

After getting off the bus at Gwynn Oak, we walked a short distance to the park's gates, with all of us chattering about the day. You could see the sloped layout of the land. I can still feel the excitement of seeing what was ahead of me. My eyes were on the old Merry-go-round located straight down the hill. The constant music coming from it made everything seem cheerful and breezy. It was like being on a memorable adventure to me every time. On the right side was an arcade, and at the entrance was a coin-operated robotic-looking gypsy lady; she looked dusty and old. For a nickel, she would turn her head, and with an extending hand, she would offer advice in the form of a small card called a Radiogram, which came out of the side of the machine. There were picture booths and one interesting one called a Voice-O-Graph booth, where we made a record. That was futuristic to me, and we had it at Gwynn Oak Park.

Voice-O-Graph record made May 1954, Radiogram card

The Dixie Ballroom, located in Gwynn Oak Park, was a famous dance hall in the late 1940s and early 1950 was considered a fancy place to go. The attire was suits and dresses. Just picture the dance floor with dancers moving to the big band sound and jitterbug. As time went by, the 1950s became a rock and roll soul-style sound. The 1960s came, and there was a change of venue. The radio station WFBR, a Baltimore AM radio station did live broadcasts from the ballroom on acre park at the corner of Gwynn Oak Park and Gwyndale Avenues are about a quarter-mile off Liberty Heights Avenue. The amusement park existed from 1893 until 1973. The attractions were slowly disappearing with a lack of customers. The flooding of the Gwynn Falls River and hurricane Agnes sealed the park's fate. With the new zoning The park was considered a flood plain of today's world, and rebuilding was not allowed and not wanted. It was a place that created memories with my friends and me. In 1974 rides were auctioned off, and the Merry go Round (Carousel) is located now at the National Mall in Washingon D, C. Today, the land is now a picnic ground.

Scarf and bobby-pin beauties Gwynn Oak Park photos-left to the right – Janet - Jackie - Raya 1956 Happy Times and happy to say Jackie and I are still friends.

GOODBY GWYNN OAK PARK 1974

In the 1940s, 1950s, and into the 1960's Bethlehem Steel was the largest employer in the city. Founded in 1887 as Maryland Steel, who built tug boats, dredges, cargo ships, passenger ships, and destroyers and was renamed Bethlehem Shipbuilding Corporation in 1916 after being purchased by Baltimore Marine Industries. In the late 1950s, Between Sparrow's Point and the Shipyard employed more than 45,000 workers.

AAUBREY BODINE

Sparrows Point 1945, Steel Mill just a memory now.

The end of a lifestyle for Baltimoreans and employment. No more buses filled with guys with stained, Sweaty, dirty clothing, thermos, lunch boxes, and the smell and sight of a hard day's work. The East Monument Street bus was for the Shipyard at Curtis Point. Several blocks away were the Fayette Street bus to the Steel Mill. Working at Sparrows Point and the shipyard those days was like earning a badge of honor for the war effort, and later it was a good union and a steady job. Many times there were 3 to 4 buses at one time to pick up the workers for the steel mill, it would be standing room only or wait till the next bus comes. The Bethlehem Fairfield Shipyard opened in 1941, located on the south shore of the Middle River Branch of the Patapsco River, which served as the Baltimore Harbor. This shipyard was one of two emergency shipyards established by the Maritime Commission under the Emergency Shipbuilding program in 1941 to help with theWorld War 11 effort.

During those five years, the shipyard employed 27,000 people. The yard closed in 1945 because the Baltimore Harbor was so old (Dating back to 1706) that the area did not have enough space for a shipway and a fabrication plant in the same waterfront area.

PHOTO COURTESY OF AAUBREY BODINE

Key Highway, 1955. Fascinating picture. Wow, sights we will never see again. Check out the oil slicks.

The shipyard is now the underground entrance for the Baltimore Harbor Tunnel. What a significant era for that generation. They were the builders of this nation. The final blow for Sparrows Point happened in January 2015; the implosion of the "L" blast furnace ended the chapter of a steel mill in Baltimore and the end of steel production for most of the United States.

PHOTO COURTESY OF AAUBREY BODINE

Bethlehem – Fairfield – Liberty Ship, 1940's, moving out from shipyard with help from two tugboats.

Another gone landmark is the Bethlehem Fairfield Shipyard. They built the Liberty ships that were mass-produced cargo ships built to meet the United States' maritime transport needs. Above is an excellent picture of a Liberty ship, which gives us a good idea of what this country built at one time These ships built in nine months alone are incredible, and there were many others to follow. President Roosevelt said that this new class of ships would bring liberty to Europe, giving rise to the name "Liberty ship." SS Patrick Henry 's maiden voyage had various armaments, including a 4-inch deck gun and an assortment of anti-aircraft guns. What else we will probably never know. During World War II, she made 12 voyages to ports, including Murmansk (as part of a convoy), Trinidad, Cape Town, Naples, and Dakar.

On September 27, 1941, called Liberty Fleet Day, the first 14 ships, including the SS Patrick Henry, were launched, all in one day. That alone is amazing.

The shipyard workers with 3 or 4 shifts seriously wanted to win the war. She survived the war but was severely damaged when she went aground on a reef off Florida's coast in July 1946, scrapped in Baltimore in 1958. The Liberty ships and the shipbuilding yard are gone, but what an incredible sight that must have been. Made in Baltimore. Ripples

The Inner Harbor is now a tourist attraction, historic seaport, and landmark in Baltimore. It was a neighborhood at one time. I remember when I was small visiting this area, and even at that time, the district was very old. Some buildings were from the 1800s. There were row houses that seemed small. The stairways were very narrow. Those tiny houses were 13 feet wide. There were some manufacturing businesses still in the 1940s and 1950s, like Domino Sugar Refinery at Locust Point, an entire neighborhood surrounded by an industrial circle, which was initially Polish, Italian and Irish immigrants. Pratt Street Power Plant, McCormick Spice Plant on Light Street, Allied Signal Chromium Plant, W. G Scarlett Seed Company. At that time, Baltimore docks and wharves were still being used on Light Street; there was shipping activity. Before Inner Harbor, Baltimore still had a working harbor for shipping and steamboats. In the 1950s, The city demolished the piers, and other cities realized that those times were over. In the early 1960s, there was one remaining steamboat at pier one. It is hard to believe that Ocean Liners once docked there. In the previous years, it was a place where European ship line terminals welcomed the new immigrants first to step foot in America. It was the beginning of building industrial America. A sight that must have been was people from other lands coming to become American citizens and create a new life, all for the love of their new country. Our city of communities and our neighborhoods were born. Inner Harbor was once the 2nd leading Port of Entry and a major manufacturing center. Fells Point had the most profound point for that natural harbor. Tabacco from the Engish trade, coffee ships from Brazil, the construction of clipper ships, and just think of how it was, a world away from what it is now. The thick black smoke from the vessel was a regular sight, along with the smell of diesel. I'm sure it had its share of local small corner bars, the old fashion social clubs, and one restaurant that stands out was Conneleys. They were famous for their oysters. You could not get any fresher; after all, they came from their back yard, the bay.

Many ripples happened during the years; the most weighty were the conflicts and wars during that period. This affected life, men going to work, men leaving home to fight, and many never return. Women working in areas where they were never allowed to before, some women had to be moms and Dad. The feminist movement was starting in a new light.

On December 7, 1941, the United States declared war on Japan, even though World War 11 was going on for quite some time over in Europe, after the bombing and destruction of our naval base, Pearl Harbor, Hawaii. It became inevitable that we must join the fight against Japan and Hitler Germany. In France, in May 1945, there was an unconditional surrender of Germany at Reims. Japan refused to surrender, and in August 1945, President Harry S. Truman gave the ok for the use of the atomic bomb on Hiroshima, Japan. Three days later, the second bomb dropped on Nagasaki, Japan. Several days later, the Japanese surrendered. Human catastrophic for all.

Waiting for their loved ones fighting during World War II, 1942.

These small flags with a little fringe on the bottom were a sign of support for the soldiers. This one has an anchor and the inscription U.S.Navy.

George Koerner on the way to France Year 1941 Paris 1941

Postcard mailed from France to 408 North Port
Street Year 1944 Beautiful artwork

Well, that was the 1940's 1950 brought a new time and a new war. On June 25, 1950, the Korean War began. North Korean troops invaded South Korea. The United States got involved after this incident. In 1953 the fighting stops in Korea. The United Nations Command, including the United States and other combatants, North Korea and China, signed an armistice agreement.

During that time, all Schools had air-raid drills. We got under the desk for our protection, so we were told. Sometimes it was a little frightening for a small child; you were a child; nothing needed to be explained to you.

The 1960s had their war; the Vietnam war started in 1964, and the United States had military advisors on the ground since 1955. This war was a different kind of fighting; it was jungle warfare, and all those young men sent over there to fight in an unknown land were at a disadvantage. This horrible war became real after hearing of our friends killed in a foreign land. Some came back; they were not the same. In 1966 more than 445,300 brave American troops were fighting this war. Several hundred thousand Americans died during this Conflict. The rest is history from 1955-to 1975. In 1965 the first public burning of a Draft card happened in protesting the Vietnam War. Done by a group of students, the group called National Coordinating Committee To end The War In Vietnam. This war was unpopular. In the past wars and conflicts, now the horrors were exposed and seen thru the new type of news media and access to the fighting areas. In the past, our country shrouded the dead from the average citizen. The most information the people were getting in World War 11 and the Korean War was a letter several weeks old, and a movie theatre newsreel showing picked over subjects.

During the Viet Nam war, access changed, and the tragic facts of war were more exposed. We saw many coffins being taken off large transport planes and lined up in an airplane hanger for family pickup. I know that sounds awful, but that is the truth. War is horrendous. It changed neighborhoods and families forever. This sorrowfulness will continue as long as there is war.

BLOODLETTING MARINE BRINGS SOUVENIRS OF WAR
Cpl. Carter shows knife and jungle hat from Vietnam

Marine Scout on Leave

Sniper Aims at 'Charlies'

Local hero, in the year 1967, my cousin, Ronnie Coster, was a primary reconnaissance sniper and team leader. During his two tours in Viet Nam, Ron received numerous military awards. Some of these include the title of E-6 Staff Sergeant, a Presidential Unit Citation, service with three stars, an award for National Defense, Good Conduct, and Expeditionary Service. He was most proud of his Purple Heart, which he received on June 2, 1966, after being seriously wounded in combat and was left with scars during contact with communist insurgent forces at Cam Lo in the Republic of South Vietnam. Ronnie passed on September 28, 2018. Let's never forget these men and women and the tremendous sacrifice they made that affected the rest of their life. I only wish Ronnie lived long enough to see his face in my book and know how proud I am of my cousin.

During the most challenging times, Baltimoreans liked to frequent the local bars, saloons, and supper clubs. It seemed to be every other corner. The neighborhood hangouts with beer, liquor, food, and local conversations. In the local row house corner bars, children had to enter at the side or back door. The décor was a long and narrow room. There were shiny gold-colored spittoons on the floor, one for every barstool. If you don't know what it is, it was the container into which tobacco chewers spit. There were other ways of disposing of all that spit and other things; in some bars, below the barstool railings, the footrest was a trough, and at the end of the bar was a faucet to turn the water on so the pipe could get flushed. The lighting was dim; on top of the bar were local delicacies in large jars with red-hot sausages, pickled eggs, pickles, and sour onions.

Purchase a Pepsi, sour onion, or pick up an order for someone. There was a time you could have your pint or quart container with a lid for purchasing beer for takeout or raw oysters.

Pint and quart containers used in the 1920s made of Porcelain

Down the alley on Orleans and Port Street alley was the local corner Dieter's bar. The bartender was Mr.Lynch, a longtime resident, was quite a character, had a deep, scary voice, and could give a look, and he knew everyone and where they lived, so no misrepresenting. Most of these small bars seemed like one on every other corner, had kitchens in the rear, and served dinners like sour beef and dumplings. It was another culturally familiar smell in the neighborhood.

Even though some of these buildings still exist, the cultural sights, sounds, and smells are no longer present. But it was not just local bars that were open for business during World War 11 and till around the mid-fifties. Scattered thru out the city was the supper clubs/nightclubs. In the 1940s, George and Vietta Koerner enjoyed a cocktail now and then. The Blue Mirror located at 929 North Charles Street, the Walnut Grove located on 3612 Hanover Street, and the most popular The Club Charles on Charles and Preston Streets. Club Charles closed in 1951; this was a classy place, with table cloths, ashtrays, coat and hat checker, a photographer for pictures, music, and a show with dinner. I think I would love for that to come back.

Club Charles Year 1940's, styles and sights

Club Charles early 1940's

In the 1940s and early 1950, the city's lighting was quite different from today. The lamp post was essential for playing game tag, red light, and dare you because that old victorian green lamppost was always home base. When that light came on, it was a sign for us to get home.

Imagine gas lights in the entire city of Baltimore. How visually beautiful; it had its safety problems, but that yellow glow seemed to put a blush of luminosity in the surrounding area.

PHOTO COURTESY OF AABODINE

Do I remember and forget or never notice how it looked when the snow would fall around that glowing yellow globe. It was of no interest then. Now I am older, and there is still a yearning in my heart and wishing I had taken that extra look.

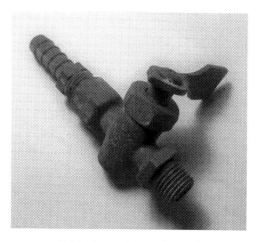

Original gas value, maybe 1906?

The gas lights for both streets and houses. The old gas value was sticking out of the wall by the kitchen stove in my Grandmother's house on Port Street. There were still gas lights at the end of world war II, and in the early 1950s, the conversion to mercury vapor lamps happened.

Mayor Thomas D'Alesandro put out the last gas light on August 14, 1957. His daughter Nancy Pelosi, Speaker of the House, grew up on Albemarle Street in Little Italy. At the same time, I lived in East Baltimore. I have to say she was born March 1940, a year before me. She was a member of St. Leo's Church. Even though we were on opposite sides of the tracks. I wonder if we ever crossed paths.

In 1957, Lamplighters were no longer necessary, and before the timers, men would walk through the streets, hauling ladders and climbing up the poles. Physically turning off the lamps at dawn and turning them on at dusk. The city recycled old gas lamps, some at Disneyland, Cape May, New Jersey, and who knows where else. I wonder if I will or did pass by my old neighborhood street light, that would be something.

PHOTO COURTESY OF AABODINE

Sights of the old gas lights and the lamplighter. There was a song in 1950, The old Lamplighter, by the Browns. This lamplighter's name is Walter Lindman. On August 4, 1957, at Bruce and Lemon Street.

PHOTO COURTESY OF AAUBREY BODINE

A frequent sight during the 1940s and early 1950s, the Streetcleaner with his shovel, broom, and his creaky cart made of wood, trashcan inside.

Gas stations and repair garages were few and far between. Most of them were rowhouses located in the middle of a block. John's Body Service at 1830 North Milton Avenue with room for one car.

Chapter Thirteen

THE FRONT STEP SETTERS

A tribute to the neighborhood's people

The front steps were more than a platform to go to your destination; they were much more than that. Does this sound like some old science fiction going on? Steps were no space ships, but perhaps something more central, a sounding board, a podium, and a familiar feeling of contentment. In Baltimore and many other cities and small towns before the Internet, cell phones, and widespread use of main landlines. The steps, solid objects, were involved in a mental and social relationship with people, the constant sound of communication between neighbors and friends; they were relating thoughts and ideas. Philosophies, beliefs, opinions, viewpoints, negotiations, mindsets, and dreams, along with joyfulness, sorrows, and sometimes accepted wisdom from the older generation, the speed of that information was so fast they might as well have a wire connected to it. The social connection gave us a feeling of belonging at that time; what else could it be? Call it just chatting, talking, conversation, resolve, speaking, yak, discussion, exchange, dialog, only sitting on the steps. It was prolific. Would it be too strange to say that we lived in the middle of a spider web, and like spiders, we could feel the vibrations of the center expanding out?

Explanation: Connection. The people who sat on those steps and would stroll around the neighborhood and converse with the step sitters were all on a journey of being social humans and part of the community. That's what made it work. Like old vinyl records that seem to be a little scratchy but still heard, most of the photos in this chapter are not digital or professionally done but are in their natural state, some grainy and worn. The conclusion is that these people were there and left a footprint. They are not visible anymore, they are in the photos, and I can feel their presence. And hopefully, you too.

They will be forgotten and somewhat unable to be recalled to mind; they endured hard times and still survived, caring for and respecting their neighborhood. The majority were the low working class, with limited education. Going to high school was sometimes impossible. Some were able to pursue higher education; this was not easy. Some were heading to the middle class, some not, and some lost the way and never recovered. It was a neighborhood of hard work, pride, and the stubbornness inherited from our Ancestors. I felt that I had to write our story. It's our History.

PHOTO COURTESY OF AA BODINE

The year 1945

Brown soap, spic and span, scrub brush, water, rag, bucket, elbow grease.

This photo is one of the most iconic scenes at that time in the city. A specialized and proud Baltimore Tradition, every Saturday, it was my job to scrub the steps.

Encompassed are pictures of step sitters, and others, different decades, different styles, but all belonging to a unique club, the Neighborhood.

Oldest photo of Port street-front steps, the year 1908, George Koerner

In the 1940s, many young men left home to fight World War II in Europe, and there were young women were waiting on the front steps for their soldiers to come home.

Vietta was my Aunt married to my uncle George Koerner. I found this old picture above in my Uncle's belongings and kept it. Now I know why he left it for me; it was to share this beautiful moment in time on the front steps.

*In the year 1945, Joanne D tricycle rode on North
Rose, loved the old shutters with hooks*

*In the year 1949, at 2400 Block East Jefferson Street,
neighbors and friends Richard, Mary Ellen, and Joey*

Early 1950's Port Street Ball and Jacks

Early 1950's First pair of sandals and neighbor Charles

Miss Baltimore Year 1961, Christmas with snow Port Street

Easter was a favorite time to take photos on the sunny side of the street in 1963

Port Street cutie with band-aid 1959 The Jefferson Street step sitter gang

People

More 1940's Dress up days

A visit from Uncle George on leave from France 1942

Stylish, back yard 408 North Port Street, behind the
fence was the huge Bowen pigeon coop

This photo is what they use to call double focus. It frequently happened with the old cameras.
North Collington Avenue, the 1940s. No special effects are needed here. I love it

Grandmom and Grandpop Sunday dress for church

1900 block North Bradford Street Easter.
Easter Best for Doris.

Stella, a lady with many talents, self-
taught, playing piano at age 7.
A Mom, and the local east Baltimore
tavern piano player and singer

Best Buds Easter Year 1946 Still best buds, Bobby pins,
ponytail, and rolled dungarees (now called jeans)

Janet and Richard Year 1955

City style 1950s Coat called toppers Elvina Styling George

Richard making a statement North Port Street Year 1950's

East Jefferson Street Joanne and Helen sporting
peddle pushers Year 1950's Joanne

In the year 1950's North Collington Avenue Sharp dresser, Zoot suit,
pegged pants with Cuban heels. Cool Dude Doc Hunt and friends

In the year 1950's Monument Street Front of John Hopkins Hospital

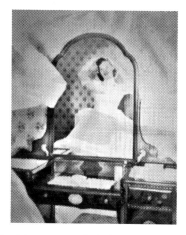

Doris is getting ready for her 1950s wedding

2400 block East Jefferson Street Home décor of the day, how's that wallpaper?

1950s Neighborhood Meeting

1950's Queen of the times, Pepsi and chips

Hanging out at the park, short shorts, and flowers in Jackie's hair, City baseball
D.A. hairstyle on left 1950s

1962 left to right: David, Irvin, Richard, and Albert. Easter Sunday. At Jefferson Pharmacy
on North Montford Avenue and East Jefferson Street, Best Buds and sharp dressers

Terri of North Collington Avenue 1958 Redbrick, form stone,
marble steps, and painted screens equaled Baltimore

Madeline, Granddaughter, Great-granddaughter, and Great-
grandson. The last of our Port Street step-sitters

1990

The end of an era for the Koerner descendants and ancestors. Madeline Vanik was born in this house in 1912. Now must leave; the change was too much for her. She was one of many who tried to make a go of it, hoping for the best. A feeling of great sorrow for her. Those steps have had five generations sitting on them. She mulled over this decision until the day she died.

PHOTO COURTESY OF CHARLES ROBINSON

Eager Street and Collington Avenue with St. Wenceslaus in the background show a stormy time. Gone is a thriving community with people and local traffic always constant. This ghostly and remarkable imageis by Charles Robinson with an appropriate title, A Street That No Longer Exist.

CHANGE

Chapter Fourteen

THE BURYING PLACE

Neighborhood Cemeteries

Tombstones
To gaze at a piece of rock
With fixed names and dates
We feel a human presence
How is that feeling possible?
On this cold earthen object
There is the absence of a soul
Even so, our focus is to feel them there
And feel a small piece of their spirit
We are truly spiritual beings
Written July 2018 Author: Janet Divel nee Vanik

Just as there were neighborhood schools, grocery stores, and churches, the neighborhood Funeral Homes and cemeteries were just as important. Traditionally, people would visit their deceased relatives on Holidays and birthdays, flowers are put on the gravesite to show remembrance. The walk was never too far for visiting the cemeteries at any time was the norm—a significant slice of our culture, which is now gone. For three days and two viewings a day, all the family and friends would attend and linger in the Funeral Parlor till all the guests were gone. In our east Baltimore neighborhood, there were several Funeral homes. The local funeral home was on 2334 East Jefferson Street, established in 1896 by John Miller. The successor of the business was Hartley Miller Jr.

This business was on the corner of Jefferson Street and North Montford Avenue, located in an 18-foot wide corner row house. Also local was the Schimunek Funeral Home on 2601-05 East Madison Street. The funeral directors and their families lived on the second floor with the viewing parlor was on the first floor. The preparation area was in the Basement.

There were other ways of viewing. There came a time I learned the different protocols and how other people honored their dead. It happened when I lost a playmate at the age of nine. The parlors of some homes would serve as a funeral viewing area. The neighbors, including the children, had to pay their respects. Meaning kneeling at the coffin and saying a prayer. No matter how old you were.To enter his home that day, I had to give myself a push. The front room had a dreary light flickering. I remember the shadows in the room and hearing sobs from the corners. The house had that strong candle burning smell like a church. It was my turn to pay my respects. I looked at his face, pale white with no smile. I had many bouts of confusion growing up, trying to understand where is that perfect world, soon realize it was not here. I could not understand again why someone I cared about was gone. I figured it out after a while. I had to. I still have vivid memories of that experience. Sometimes a good memory is a curse. After that, I took a shortcut around the block to avoid that house.Life insurance benefits or policies were not as available as today. More than not, most people did not have life insurance. Sometimes the alternative plan was home viewings. There were cases where the family members paid what they could afford to funeral parlors. Being a low-income area, they knew that they were part of the neighborhood and acted suitably. When my older brother passed, Mr. Miller came to our home and had a conversation with my mother about the expenses. Those city neighbors, including some business owners who understood the area and the people.

During the late 1800s and early 1900s, the churches were building cemeteries at a fever pitch. On 4453 Belair Road, across from the Most Holy Redeemer Cemetery, was the Keller's Beloved Memorials, Inc., They were the east Baltimore stonemasons. It closed its doors in the 1990s. The vandalism and the change of the culture made them no longer viable in the area.

Most of my ancestors are at the Most Holy Redeemer Cemetery. The cemetery was a member of the Redemptorist order. Many local churches were of that order. This cemetery at 4300 Belair road was for members of the Catholic faith. Sixty acres opened in May 1882 in the Gardenville area, and a dark stone, narrow round entrance on Belair Road, later stuccoed over. The stone (below) entrance and building in the 1980s, you can see a dark stone on the side of the Building that's was the old facade.

1980's

The noticeable feature of this cemetery is the Furst Chapel on the high part of the property. This chapel was donated by Mr. and Mrs. Frank Furst and are interred along with 61 members of the Redemptorist order. The records are at the office of the Sacred Heart of Jesus Cemetery. Cemeteries are visual history books.

The Furst Chapel 2018

A nine-year-old child's beheaded tombstone slowly
slipping into the earth dated 1916

The Most Holy Redeemer Cemetery 2018 My family burying ground

Rolling hills and stone with carvings frozen in time.
Most Holy Redeemer Cemetery The year 2018

July 2018 Belair Road and Moravia Avenue

Belair Road and Moravia Avenue, the old stone fence versus metal fence. It's sad when they have to keep out people alive and do not have the best intentions during their cemetery visits. As a child, my friends and I found a play area or thought it was a place to explore at Biddle Street and Edison Hwy. A small concrete building on that hillside with a rusty metal collapsed door. There were odd-shaped rocks, but the weeds and small trees made it unclear what they were. There came a time when a story came out saying that a girl was found dead on that lot, and that was the end of the exploring. I know now It was an abandoned cemetery, and it was where we played in the early 1950's, many lost souls, and there were 2,431 remains there. We had no idea. This property was the St Alphonsus Cemetery, originally named St. Michaels burying grounds, opened in the year 1850, closed in 1917 and was abandoned. It was 17 acres, and the city purchased the property in 1961. According to city records, in 2010, all remains were removed to The Most Holy Redeemer Cemetery.

The Bohemian National Cemetery. At one time, called the Oak Hill Cemetery.

In 1854, Bohemian immigrants formed a benevolent organization called the C.S.P.S. that would provide activities and services and continue their history, provide health insurance, and have a cemetery for their members. For some time, serving the community, but as time went by, the leaders aged, and membership declined. In the history of this cemetery, the Czechs used this as a school and as a place where neighbors and friends would get together, sing folk songs, and eat traditional Czech food. Also, the site was for Sokol sports events. In 1884 the cemetery was dedicated by the Grand Lodge C.S.P.S. In Czech (Cesko Slovanska Podporujici Spolecnost). This cemetery consists of 12.4 acres, and there are over 3,000 burials. The Bohemian National Cemetery is now on the National Register of Historic Places as of November 11, 2010.

Caretakers Cottage

View of tombstones at the cemetery

The door of the Carriage house

As the Bohemians were building their Bohemian cemeteries and societies in 1884, the Polish immigrants 1875 organized The St. Stanislaus Societies. Like the Bohemians in the area, the Polish immigrants wanted to help and aid their newly arrived counterparts with their acclimating to America. They were called mutual aid societies and were in great need during the Depression of the 1870s. The Polish that came to Baltimore mainly were unskilled workers who worked in the Baltimore ports, slaughterhouses, and canning industries. Most lived with their family and friends who previously came over, or the churches would step in. Boarding houses were famous. If they could rent a room without signing a leasing agreement. They settled in Fells Point around 1868 thru 1880. They made a life for their families thru their hard work. In 1892 the Rev. Joseph Skretny, pastor of the St. Kostka church, bought 42 acres for a park-like setting for the children, but it soon became a burial site with over 2,000 burials. The St. Stanislaus Cemetery is located at 6515 Boston Street 21224, between Dundalk Avenue and Steelton Avenue, the O'Donnell Heights neighborhood, 2 miles from the Bohemian Cemetery.

St. Stanislaus Cemetery 2018

There seemed to be an abundance of catholic cemeteries in this area. Others are Scared Heart of Mary Cemetery is located at 7501 German Hill Road, and Sacred Heart of Jesus Cemetery is located at 7401 German Hill Road. Sacred Heart of Mary is a smaller cemetery located next to the Sacred Heart of Jesus. A total of 52 acres of farmland were purchased by the German Redemptorist Fathers around 1860 for the Sacred Heart of Jesus. In this cemetery, they allowed non-Catholics for burial. Before this cemetery, the deceased of the Sacred Heart Parish were in the St. Alphonsus Cemetery. bought by the city in 1961 and the remains moved to The Most Holy Redeemer Cemetery. Dundalk neighborhood.

Sacred Heart of Mary cemetery 2018

Sacred Heart of Jesus cemetery 2018

Holy Rosary Cemetery 2018

Located at 7305 German Hill Road,21222, from 1889. The Holy Rosary Parrish church is located at 408 South Chester Street, 21231. Initially for Catholic polish members.

Holy Rosary Cemetery 2018

Every cemetery seems to have at least one beautiful feature. So can we say this looks like Heaven's door?

Holly Cross Polish National Catholic Cemetery 2018

This entrance is the Holy Cross Polish National Catholic Cemetery, established in 1898. Another name is the Polish National Catholic Church cemetery. Located in Dundalk at 7110 German Hill Road. The Historic Parrish Holy Cross Church, located at 208 South Broadway, the Fells Point neighborhood, advertised as a One, Holy, Catholic, Apostolic, and Democratic parish. If my information is correct, they still follow traditional polish holidays and have dinners in the parish hall.

Green Mount Cemetery is on the Historic Register of Historic Places in 1980. Located at 1501 Green Mount Avenue 21222 opened in 1939. Green Mount, along with the Baltimore cemetery, is probably the most well-known. Buried here are many prominent Baltimore area families and famous people, including John Wilkes Booth, who assassinated Abraham Lincoln, John Hopkins, the founder of the John Hopkins University and Hospital, and many more. Green Mount Cemetery consists of 60 acres, a beautiful and well-maintained cemetery, despite the area's decay.

Green Mount Cemetery, What a gothic look. I did not see any gargoyles

There is a Baltimore City Landmark Plaque posted at the entrance. dedicated in 1939 to the former country estate of Robert Oliver.

At the beginning of the "rural cemetery movement, Green Mount was Baltimore's first such rural cemetery and one of the first in the United States. The campaign began as a response to the health hazard posed by overcrowded church graveyards and as part of the larger Romantic movement of the mid-1800s, which glorified nature and appealed to emotions. Green Mount reflects the romanticism of its age, not only by its very existence but also by its buildings and sculptures. The Gateway, designed by Robert Cary Long Jr. The hilltop chapel, designed by J. Rudolph Niemsee and J. Crawford Neilson, is Gothic Revival, a romantic-style medieval building. Nearly 65,000 people are buried here, including the poet Sydney Lanier, philanthropists John Hopkins and Enoch Pratt, Napoleon Bonaparte's sister-in-law Betsy Patterson, John Wilkes Booth, and numerous military, political, and business leaders."

Green Mount Cemetery, eerie gray 2018

The Front entrance 2018, Welcome

The John Wilkes Booth Family Plot

With John Wilkes Booth, two other plotters in the assassination of Abraham Lincoln are there, Samuel Arnold and Michael O'Laughlen. One of the traditions was leaving a one-cent coin with the likeness of President Lincoln. Placed on each grave of the three men who murdered him.

Green Mount Cemetery: two of its many statues create an outdoor art gallery.

How beautifully sad and serene.

The Baltimore Cemetery is at 2400 East North Avenue and North Rose Street. It is on a hilltop, quite unusual for the city.

Another gothic type on the top of the hill 2018

A view of the downtown as you stroll this cemetery, Peacefulness. The site is in a decrepit area of the city. Opened in 1850, it included 100 acres. It was more like the poor man's cemetery than the Greenmount cemetery was. Most people who reside in this place were german descendants who lived and worked in the area, including many breweries and factories located in the area. The working man's cemetery for the times.

View of downtown Baltimore 2018 tilted tombstones, angel praying to heaven. A remnant from the past and a new image of now.

In East Baltimore, there were also Hebrew Cemeteries, mainly in the Dundalk neighborhood. On 6842 German Hill Road, there is the Workers Circle Cemetery. It was a small cemetery located inside a larger one but had a specific entrance. Rowhouses and tombstones share this space.

2018
The Hebrew Friendship Cemetery at 3600 East Baltimore Street 21218. Purchased in 1849 and one of the best keep cemeteries.

The Hebrew Mount Carmel Cemetery at 5712 O'Donnell
Street 21224. Open in around 1854.

Used at one time by the Workers Circle Cemetery. This cemetery, according to the info, is in terrible shape. The tombstones are barely visible and covered with bushes and trees in the older section. It is said to be part of lost Maryland, and there are hopes that there can be a solution for this destruction.

The Oheb Shalom Cemetery Memorial Park is located at 6313 O'Donnell Street, 21224, and is in good condition.

The Hebrew Free Burial Society Cemetery at 6820 German Hill Road. This society started in 1869, and it provides burial for Jewish people in the Baltimore City area, it was and is used mainly for families who cannot pay for a plot or individuals who have no family?

Hebrew Free Burial Society Cemetery from 1908 front entrance 2018

As I took this picture, I noticed a needle down by my feet, the type used to inject drugs. It's a moment when you say; this is what's going on? The realization that this is the real world and how sad we have become.

As you look thru the front gate, there is a feeling of loneliness and poverty. Nothing fancy here; it is here for a reason and does serve its purpose.

There are many more cemeteries that were an essential part of the infrastructure of the emerging city. The cemetery was a necessary part of our ancestor's life and death and how they relied on their religious beliefs to get them thru their lifecycle and to know that they would rest in their neighborhood cemetery. As time goes by, these old cemeteries are undergoing abandonment in one way or the other. Our ancestors, who most of us did not know, are gone and have been for some time.

Neighborhoods change; they are not the same traditions that were going on in the past. How to keep These places, as part of our history, are a challenge. These places have an appeal to certain people. They can open thought for a particular type of history. The people of the past are relevant; we cannot forget their sacrifices, their lives, and that they were living beings walking down our streets, leaving invisible footprints and produced a new generation of what we are today. Everyone has their own story and family history.

Writing this story has been a very emotional journey with sadness, joy, and unexpected paths of thought. This chronicle has come to an end at this moment in time. Who knows what will be? I can only imagine the future. Knowing our history induces unique memories, stories of people and their journeys.

This book is just a tiny peek into the past of one beloved neighborhood, along with the sights, sounds, smells, and people thru photos and stories unique to that time and place. Writing this immersed me into my past, and along with that came all the memories and realizing that sometimes we lose track of ourselves. The happy ones I laugh, and the sad ones I cry. But I would never disown any of those times. If this is part of being idealistic, I am ok with that. There are times we must look thru the younger eye with our older thoughts and keep going. Always remembering we are responsible for embracing the past and assuring the future. After all, it's part of the human experience, and it does not always matter whether we live our dream, but how we go about it, and we do our best of what we understand thru life.

Put aside Yesterday
What if you could
Yesterday is who you are
You might forget the best part of you
Written by: Janet Divel nee Vanik July 2018